# STEPFAMILIES

## THE STEP BY STEP MODEL OF BRIEF THERAPY

*Mala S. Burt*

*&*

*Roger B. Burt*

BRUNNER/MAZEL, *Publishers* • New York

**Library of Congress Cataloging-in-Publication Data**

Burt, Mala Schuster.
    Stepfamilies: the step by step model of brief therapy / Mala S. Burt &
Roger B. Burt.
        p.   cm.
    Includes bibliographical references and index.
    ISBN 0-87630-832-9
    1. Family psychotherapy.  2. Stepfamilies—Counseling of.
3. Stepfamilies—Psychological aspects.  4. Brief psychotherapy.
I. Burt, Roger B.  II. Title.
RC488.5.B815   1996
616.89'156—dc20                                                                96-32988
                                                                                      CIP

*Published by*
BRUNNER/MAZEL, INC.
19 Union Square West
New York, New York 10003

Manufactured in the United States of America

10   9   8   7   6   5   4   3   2   1

To our children, Thomas, Justine, Ted, and Kira,
who continue to enrich our lives.

And to the many families with whom we worked,
who enriched our understanding of how to best assist stepfamilies.

# Contents

# Foreword

Shortly after our becoming professionally interested in working with stepfamilies, Mala and Roger Burt contacted us, and we were excited to learn of their interest in this area of therapy. Over the past 15 years, we have been keenly aware of their "Step By Step" clinic and the fine work they have been doing.

In 1980 every seventh child was thought to be a stepchild. Today, demographers predict that one third of all children born during the 1980s will live with a stepparent before their eighteenth birthday and that by the year 2010, there will be more stepfamilies than any other type of family in the United States. As a result, an increasing number of individuals seeking therapy are from this type of family, and therapists are being called upon to deal with complicated issues and strong emotions that arise in this more complex family form. Fortunately, during recent years, there has been an increasing number of excellent stepfamily research projects and a number of professional books and papers written to provide therapists with helpful information for working successfully with stepfamily individuals and family members.

At the present time, therapists are faced with practice questions of many kinds. With the advent of managed care and the current focus on accountability and authorization for therapy services, the need for accurate assessment and brief therapy has become critical to clinical practice. Fortunately, Mala and Roger Burt have been concerned over the years with assessment and evaluation of the efficacy of their therapy contacts. They have recorded demographic and clinical data on approximately 500 stepfamilies, and they have used this information together with their own personal stepfamily experience and professional expertise to outline an assessment and brief treatment system for use with stepfamilies. This has provided them with an approach that they have personally developed, tested, and proved to be effective.

The Burts' book deals with the very basic nuts and bolts of helping stepfamilies. In their words, "The assumption of normalcy drives our approach," an assumption that helps to counteract the many negative messages coming from society as well as from unknowledgeable therapists and counselors. They work initially with the couple, helping them to gain a realistic picture of stepfamily progress towards integration, to determine on what "chunks" of their life it is worth expending their energy, and to find ways in which they can be helpful to each other and to their children. It is an eminently readable book as the following quote helps illustrate:

> There is no point in spending thousands of dollars on attorneys if someone's "ex" is a drug addict or compulsive gambler and the hope of getting back child support or support on a regular basis is nil. A couple would be better advised to take the money for lawyers and go on a cruise! (p. 126)

Their assessment profile and their "Triage Management Approach" bring stepcouples a message of hope and empowerment from the very first therapy contact. Stepfamilies can feel validated and supported as they move quickly to see what needs to be dealt with and how to go about changing any "hot spots."

For approximately two thirds of the families they treated, the Burts found that short-term therapy, with an open-door policy promoting future brief contacts as the stepfamily members worked through the process of integration, to be their treatment of choice. For the remaining one third, past experiences, personality characteristics, and emotional difficulties added layers of complexity on top of stepfamily issues and required more therapy than the simple use of the Step By Step model.

The information provided by the Burts is clearly described. Indeed, for those not emotionally familiar with stepfamily living, their findings and procedures may seem simplistic and a matter of common sense already shared by most stepfamilies and therapists. However, our experience, as well as recent stepfamily research, suggest that even for many informed individuals, there is a lack of real understanding and acceptance of the situations and emotions commonly present in the average stepfamily. It is important to grasp these concepts fully since to do this can make a profound difference for therapists and for clients alike. It is important, but not easy, for this knowledge to progress from being an intellectual understanding to being a part of one's unconscious acceptance of this type of family.

We welcome this new resource. It provides a fresh look at working therapeutically with remarriage families, and both therapists and clients can benefit from reading this practical, basic, step-by-step approach to therapy and to the reduction of stepfamily chaos. We all can be thankful that Mala and Roger had the foresight to pay attention to and record the characteristics of their stepfamilies and the salient aspects of their therapy with them. We know of no one else who has engaged in this endeavor for such an extended period of time with such clarity of purpose and depth of knowledge. Thank you, Mala and Roger, for writing this book. It is a special gift for all of us.

Emily B. Visher, Ph.D.
*Adjunct Faculty*
*John F. Kennedy School of Professional Psychology*

John S. Visher, M.D.
*Lecturer in Psychiatry, Emeritus*
*Stanford University School of Medicine*

# *Acknowledgments*

Because of our longtime involvement with the Stepfamily Association of America, we have been fortunate in having access over the years to a number of people who have been enormously generous with their time, encouragement, and friendship, and who helped shape and refine our ideas about stepfamilies and how they operate. In particular, Emily and John Visher, who continue to be innovative in this evolving field; Patricia Papernow, to whom we will always be grateful for sharing her early work, and Kay Pasley, who always seemed to answer the phone when we needed the answer to a question about research.

Our thanks also to Arthur and Ruth Schwartz, whose encouragement and help in the conceptual stages of this book were instrumental in a dream becoming printed pages.

# STEPFAMILIES

# CHAPTER 1

# *Introduction*

I'm afraid that day to day life will spoil the very special relationship we have. All the kids are in turmoil; it won't be easy.

—Roger Burt, 1975

I've been raising two kids, how much harder could four be? Besides, we love each other.

—Mala Schuster, 1975

And thus began our stepfamily, created by hope and the expectation that our love and commitment would overcome any obstacles. But for us, as for many other stepfamilies, hope at times turned to confusion, resentment, and, occasionally, despair, as the reality of growing as a couple and a family took a backseat to complicated logistics, four upset children between the ages of five and eight, and dealing with former spouses. What in the world had we done?

We muddled through like most stepfamilies in the mid-seventies when no one was talking about stepfamilies. It wasn't until Roger began his private practice in 1977 and began commenting on the number of couples in second marriages he was seeing, that we began actively looking for more information about the kind of family we were creating. There was very little available.

At the beginning of our stepfamily we were largely in denial about the complications inherent in the process. After about a year, when Mala began having nightmares about protecting the family home and the children from hurricanes, tornadoes, and swarms of bees and seemed to be crying a lot, Roger suggested she see a therapist. Mala had never been in therapy, but it seemed like a good idea. The first therapist listened to all that she reported about her divorce, the recent death of her father, the upset of the children in sharing the house where Roger had lived with his first wife, and trying to feel okay about living in "another woman's home." Then there were Roger's two jobs and the fact that he was not home much to help with the children...and on and on. This therapist felt that it was a family issue and referred Mala and Roger to a family therapist.

The family therapist, at the end of the first interview, pronounced this a clear case of the family's scapegoating Mala's older son. Again, no mention of stepfamily dynamics. As we discussed the session later, this interpretation also seemed to miss the point. If anybody in the family was scapegoated, it was Mala's younger son, Ted. Thomas, the oldest of the four children, was the most vocal at that point about his unhappiness with the new living arrangements.

So Mala tried another therapist, who recommended she go into ongoing treatment because of unresolved issues about her father (who had died the year before). No mention was made of the chaos and upheaval inherent in trying to join two families. Because Mala was still sad about her father and therapy seemed like an intriguing idea, she entered a group. A year later she had learned a lot about herself, but nothing about her stepfamily situation. In fairness to these three therapists, little was known about stepfamily dynamics in the early 1970s.

We think it is interesting that when we married twenty years ago we did not think of ourselves as a stepfamily. Somehow, it just didn't come up. We were married and trying to raise four children, but didn't think of ourselves as a stepfather, stepmother, and four stepchildren inhabiting the same house. We were just a couple trying our best to recover from our divorces and raise our children.

## HOW STEP BY STEP BEGAN

Our work with stepfamilies began in something of a vacuum. Roger had a Ph.D. in Clinical Psychology from Duke University and had recently opened a private practice after a number of years as a psychologist working in Baltimore's first community mental health center. It was this work that developed his interest in crisis intervention and in the usefulness of brief interventions that capitalized on a client's strengths and resources.

Mala had a B.A. in English Literature from Goucher College and had taught briefly before taking on the more challenging role of stepmother. She later earned a Master of Social Work degree from the University of Maryland at Baltimore.

We started Step By Step because we knew what we would have wanted when our stepfamily began. We knew that stepfamilies were different from first-marriage families. We also had some ideas about social reactions to stepfamilies. Our goal was to be a resource center for stepfamilies, a place where stepfamilies could get information and support. We advertised full- and half-day workshops and groups for adults in stepfamilies, believing that educational experiences and programs offering group support would be most helpful. We anticipated a positive response from the community.

We soon learned a lot from the stepfamilies who called. Most felt that they were not yet ready for involvement in a group or workshop experience. Their pain was too intense, too raw. They needed to tell their stories privately. Many told us that they needed to feel more hopeful about their family relationships before they could share their feelings in a group setting. These stepfamilies gave us multiple insights into what they needed and how they could accept assistance. Quite a few stepfamilies told us they had been to other therapists who "put us all in a room together," sometimes with ex-spouses, and begged us not to do the same.

Many of the families who came to see us seemed to get what they needed in a few sessions. Others came intermittently, a few sessions at a time, creating the PRN (pro re nata) or "as needed" model we utilize today. These families showed us that the kind of help they needed most was intensive, issue-centered, and often crisis-related, but provided in small chunks over the long period of time it takes the stepfamily to begin to function more successfully. Some families gained enough information and support in their brief contact with us that they could be referred to a stepfamily support group or were able to proceed on their own.

Thus it was that the model evolved, based on what stepfamilies told us they needed, our own stepfamily experience, our educational and work backgrounds, our styles of working, and what we learned each day about the therapeutic strategies that worked. Our involvement as members of the national board of Stepfamily Association of America was, for us, a personal support group and a chance to talk with clinicians around the country. Most of these clinicians were, like us, personally involved in a stepfamily and also seeing stepfamily clients.

We began to talk together about what kinds of things we needed to know about the family and its members in the first session or two. Out of this grew the Stepfamily Assessment Guide and the notion of Triage Assessment, techniques designed to gather the necessary information rapidly and help couples focus their energy on constructive change. Stepfamilies let us know that they were hungry for information about their situations. What did we want to give them to help educate them about the process? How would we focus and structure the interventions? We knew we wanted to extend the influence of the therapy hour; what kind of homework assignments would we give? What kind of termination process would occur?

When we look back at our early training workshops, we can see that the assumptions we made then about what would be helpful to stepfamilies have changed very little. We did not begin to think about our model as a "brief therapy model" until recently, but it certainly fits the accepted definitions.

## The Step By Step Model

While clinicians need to attend to intrapsychic and psychodynamic factors, the Step By Step model is based on the realities of stepfamily interactions, adjustments, and development, and on our belief that traditional modes of therapy do not serve this population well. Stepfamilies are structurally different from non-remarried families. They are formed after divorce or death; there are differences in relationship histories; there is often a biological parent (ex-spouse) who continues to interact with the new family; children can be members of two or more households; stepparents are asked to assume parental roles before the relationships are established; and no legal relationship exists between some stepfamily members. Because of these and other factors, stepfamilies have special needs that must be considered by clinicians (Visher & Visher, 1988).

## Traditional Therapy Approaches

Traditional psychotherapies do not focus on the factors mentioned above, and therefore often they do not address the most pressing needs of stepfamilies. Therapists may push for family or dyadic cohesion before a stepfamily or its members are developmentally ready, or they may ask stepparents to assume parental roles too quickly. Family therapies that insist on the inclusion of all family members in the session do not support and nurture the fragile stepcouple relationship or assist the couple in choosing and implementing *appropriate and achievable* goals for change. Family therapy models that strive to increase the intensity of interactions in the session as a way of destabilizing the family system can be destructive. The stepfamily, at the point of contact with the clinician, badly needs help with stabilization, not further destabilization (Browning, 1994). We believe that the establishment of a parental hierarchy is crucial, but the stepparental hierarchy functions differently than the parental hierarchy in first marriage families where both parents are biological parents. Clinicians must be cognizant of these differences.

## Brief Treatment Model

We believe that a brief treatment model for stepfamilies is the treatment of choice, based on our fifteen years of direct client service to this population. Brief treatment models are seen as both clinically effective and cost effective.

The Step By Step model is similar to other brief therapy models. Philosophically, it is closely allied to the work of Cummings and Budman (Zeig, 1990). Cummings introduced the notion of the psychotherapist as psychological family practitioner in his serial brief therapy—a model of brief psychotherapy provided as needed throughout a person's life cycle. It featured targeted interventions and seemed to focus on crises generated by developmental changes. Therapy in Cumming's model is interrupted rather than terminated (Zeig, 1990).

Budman also describes therapy as a "resource that the patient may use and return to at many points over the life cycle" (Zeig, 1990, p. 213). While the Step By Step model is not necessarily a lifelong intervention, it clearly positions the clinician as teacher and guide to the developmental transitions of all kinds encountered by stepfamilies. And because the clinician knows the individuals in the family, he or she is in a position to make referrals for more traditional, longer-term therapies if needed.

Like many brief therapy models, the Step By Step model is process oriented, assisting clients to seek solution-focused responses to specific problems. Solutions include education that stresses reality-based observations about other stepfamilies, skill building (particularly problem solving, negotiation and compromise, family management, and communication), and building on the existing coping strengths of the family system. Goal setting is a collaborative process between client and therapist. Origins of problems are considered but are not usually the focus of the intervention.

The Step By Step brief therapy model is not rigid. Like the stepfamilies it serves, it is of necessity a flexible model, continually tailored and altered to meet the unique and changing needs of the family system being worked with. An expectation of brief therapy is set up from the initial telephone contact, when it is explained that our work with stepfamilies is usually brief because of the protracted nature of the adjustment, and that families are encouraged to use us as a resource to access other support systems and for the purpose of occasional consultation.

## CHARACTERISTICS OF THE CLINICAL POPULATION AND DURATION OF INTERVENTION

In fifteen years, we have seen close to 500 stepfamilies. Because our practice was not designed as a research study and so was not set up to collect data, the statistical data we are able to generate are limited. Unfortunately, outcome studies or follow-ups were not part of our practice. However, the data that we are able to extrapolate from case files are interesting and useful.

We have data on some aspects of our work, such as the structure of the families who came to see us, how long they stayed in treatment, presenting problems, and so on, but we do not have outcome indicators. Until recently, our clients have been almost exclusively self-referred. At the beginning of our practice we received an unusual amount of publicity in the Baltimore area, which meant that the local population knew about us and our specialty. The burgeoning influence of managed care, which prescreens and refers to its own provider panels, has changed the types of cases being referred to our office.

Our clinical population is not a random sample and may be representative only of private practice settings. Until the advent of managed care, most clients were self-referred; none court-ordered. Most are Caucasian and of middle or working class socioeconomic backgrounds. We did not collect data on income or other socioeconomic indicators. Information about types of jobs held and education level of clients is often imbedded in intake and session notes but was not collated for this book. We have some experience working with African American families (almost all middle class or upper middle class) and almost no experience with a Hispanic population or other ethnic minorities. We would be very interested to see if the strategies we found successful with our clinical population would work with other populations.

We removed the files of stepfamilies that had been seen by other therapists who occasionally have worked in the Step By Step offices because those therapists had not been trained in the Step By Step model. Thus, the samples are composed of families seen by Roger and Mala Burt. The Ns of some samples are inconsistent because all information was not always included on intake sheets, posing a tremendous problem for anyone sifting through session records. These records no doubt contain much additional data.

While no systematic research study was undertaken, there is information available that describes the characteristics of our clinical population. The data is derived from random samples from two periods. The first period, 1979 to 1987, represents a self-selected population who came for help with stepfamily problems. The second period, 1991 to 1992, has a smaller sample and reflected our curiosity about what effects the intervention of managed care in the referral process had on our stepfamily cases.

Table 1.1 shows only the results of the self-selected sample and reflects the marital status and length of the relationship of those seeking help. Over 75 percent of the couples had been married less than four years, which places them in the early stages of stepfamily development. We did not break down the data on couples who were engaged or living together to show how many years they had been together.

Table 1.2 shows characteristics of both the 1979–1987 and 1991–1992 samples described above. In almost half of the families from the earlier group, one of the partners had no children, which contributed to their distress. It can also be seen that almost three-quarters of these couples had adolescents in the home. Also, a surprising number of this sample were dealing with adult children. We came to view a number of these characteristics, when coexistent, as indications of stepfamilies who were at more risk for another marital disruption. Later in the book, we will provide a more specific discussion of the characteristics of the stepfamilies we view as most vulnerable.

The second sample, (1991–1992) shows the effect of managed care referrals on stepfamilies who presented with these characteristics. The self-selected sample and the sample referred by managed care show a distinct reversal in the first two characteristics. The most vulnerable families we saw were those where the women had no children of their own, which was true in almost one-third of the cases in the self-selected sample.

## TABLE 1.1
### Number of Years in Relationship When Help Is Sought

N=179

| Time and Status of Relationship | Percentage of Total Sample |
| --- | --- |
| Engaged and/or living together | 21.8% |
| Married less than 1 year | 17.3% |
| Married 1 year | 14.5% |
| Married 2 years | 12.8% |
| Married 3 years | 11.2% |
| Married 4 years | 6.7% |
| Married 5 years | 6.1% |
| Married 6+ years | 9.5% |

## TABLE 1.2
### Salient Characteristics of Stepfamilies Seeking Counseling

| Characteristics | N=219 1979–1987 | N=50 1991–1992 |
| --- | --- | --- |
| Men with no children from prior relationship | 14.6%[1] | 34.0% |
| Women with no children from prior relationship | 33.3%[2] | 18.0% |
| Couples in which one partner has no children from prior relationship | 47.9% | 52.0% |
| Mother has physical custody of one or more of her children[3] | 62.1% | 78.0% |
| Father has physical custody of one or more of his children | 45.6% | 26.0% |
| One of the parents has at least one teenage child | 71.2% | 76.0% |
| One of the parents has at least one adult child | 20.5% | 16.0% |

*Note:* No combination of the above will total 100%. For example, some women in the sample do not have custody of any of their children and some of these families have adult children.

[1] 6.2% of these men have children from current relationship.

[2] 26.0% of these women have children from current relationship. In almost all instances the children involved are under two years old.

[3] We consider where the children live most of the time more at issue than legal custody.

The cases referred by managed care are, in effect, a sample of stepfamilies as a whole, not the more vulnerable type of stepfamily. Apparently because people had lost their freedom of choice of provider, the most vulnerable stepfamilies could no longer seek the help of stepfamily specialists. In the second sample the families were referred not because they saw themselves as having stepfamily problems but because they showed other characteristics of disturbance.

Table 1.3 shows the length of intervention as reflected by the number of sessions. There is a clear discrepancy between the "self-selected" and "referred by managed care" samples in the number of families finishing after the first session. Over a few sessions, the discrepancy disappears. It appears that the couples in the self-selected sample were more focused on stepfamily issues and so they had selected a specific resource. The managed care sample reflects general referrals and so it was necessary to spend a session dealing with the reason for the referral. Recognition that stepfamily adjustment issues might be at the root of family problems came during the first session rather than prior to the appointment. The absence of choice and lack of differentiation of resources cost one session.

TABLE 1.3
**Cumulative Percentage of Families Finished
After a Given Number of Sessions**

| Number of Sessions | N=289 (1979–1987) | N=50 (1991–1992) |
|:---:|:---:|:---:|
| 1 | 21.8% | 8% |
| 2 | 34.3% | 20% |
| 3 | 41.2% | 32% |
| 4 | 46.4% | 42% |
| 5 | 52.9% | 48% |
| 6 | 58.8% | 52% |
| 7 | 62.6% | 60% |
| 8 | 65.7% | 64% |
| 9 | 69.2% | 68% |
| 10 | 72.7% | 72% |
| | Average number of sessions = 8.09 | Average number of sessions = 9.12 |

```
• Simple
• Collaborative
• Synergistic
• Contextual
• Process Oriented
• Cognitive
```

**Exhibit 1.1. Strengths of the Step By Step Model.**

## FOR CLINICIANS

Occasionally when we teach workshops on the Step By Step model, we are asked, "Isn't the model too simple, too superficial for such complex family issues?" We think that the strengths of this model lie in its simplicity. The fact that interventions are a collaborative effort between therapist and couple creates a useful synergy. The model views the couple in a family context, and the strong cognitive component to the intervention helps clients to feel less helpless and more in control, thus able to move forward with their lives. (See Exhibit 1.1.)

The simplicity of the model allows clinicians with different backgrounds, training, and therapeutic gifts to graft their own strengths onto it. However, they do need to have a strong knowledge base about stepfamilies so they do not inadvertently pathologize normal stepfamily processes. When stepfamilies seek professional assistance, they may encounter a lack of knowledge or understanding of stepfamily issues, and clinicians are often unprepared for the complexity of stepfamilies and the intense affect they so frequently display. Lack of understanding may result in ineffective treatment or inadvertently prolong the process by not putting stepfamily issues in perspective.

# CHAPTER 2

# The Assumption of Normalcy

The Step By Step model is focused on assisting couples and families move though the predictable stages of stepfamily development, providing them with knowledge, suggestions, and tools they would not have had if they had not consulted a stepfamily expert. The goals of this treatment model facilitate stepfamily functioning, but except by referral it does not address attempts to make changes in personality, nor does it deal with serious psychopathology.

We developed the Step By Step Model of Brief Therapy based on four assumptions we make about stepfamilies. These core assumptions are the engine that drives the model. The first of these assumptions, an assumption of normalcy about stepfamilies, provides the theoretical and philosophical foundation for this treatment model.

## ASSUMPTION #1: STEPFAMILIES ARE NORMAL FAMILIES, VALUABLE AND VIABLE IN THEIR OWN RIGHT.

The clinician using the Step By Step model assumes that stepfamilies are normal, viable, and valuable families. Unless assessment information moves treatment in another direction, the stepfamily being seen is assumed to represent a range of normal reactions to the adjustments of becoming a stepfamily.

We view stepfamilies as one of many types of families, in which people who may not be biologically related can live and grow happily and productively. We do not perceive this form of family as deviant, problem-oriented, or more likely than any other family type to be dysfunctional. Where dysfunction or problems exist, they must be addressed, but the initial assumption is that a stepfamily has the potential to be an emotionally healthy environment for family members.

## WHAT MAKES A FAMILY?

Is it blood bonds that connect families? Or is it relationship, the affinity of one to another? Are we victims of our biological imperative to keep our gene pool replicating or does our sense of family connectedness derive from the relationship constellations in which we are embedded?

Families are a complicated amalgam of blood and emotional relationships and cultural norms. Our expectations, based on these cultural norms, predict how families will function, the roles we will enact in one another's lives, and how families will provide the most basic of human needs for survival and relatedness.

The need to relate or belong to a group or family is extraordinarily strong. Most of us will do almost anything to belong because not belonging feels intolerable. Thus, belonging becomes as necessary to our survival as food and shelter. Families are our security blanket, the place we can always go when things are difficult, the place where we are accepted. And even if our life experience has shown us that we can't expect this in our families of origin, we continue to believe that this is the way it ought to be, and keep searching for home.

Emily and John Visher, who pioneered clinical work with stepfamilies, have recently begun to take an anthropological view of stepfamilies (personal conversation). They speculate that it is the feeling of being denied basic human needs such as belonging, acceptance, and nurturance that creates many of the intense feelings that arise in stepfamilies. We believe that this emotional intensity is increased for women, whose sense of self is "organized around being able to make and then to maintain affiliations and relationships" (Miller, 1976). Papernow (1994) has written at length about the importance of insider/outsider positions in the stepfamily, another way of explaining why relationships in these families become so complicated when individuals are excluded from full family participation. These fundamental ideas about basic human needs and stepfamily dynamics seem to us to be very much on target.

### Different Kinds of Families

In order to evaluate a stepfamily, we must remember that families come in many forms. As clinicians and social animals, it is often difficult to get past our own intrapsychic maps, our own emotional overlays about what constitutes a family. Our personal experiences color our perceptions and projections about what makes a "real" family. Is a single-parent family "real"? Society, along with many clinicians, views these families as "broken," apparently waiting for a husband or wife and marriage to make them whole again.

There seems to be general consensus (possibly overgeneralized and flawed) that many social ills stem from the prevalence of broken homes, a phrase seemingly synonymous with single-parent families. Does remarriage fix the problems we perceive to be prevalent in single-parent families? We believe that most people, including clinicians who have not been educated about stepfamilies, may believe this to be true.

Are gay and lesbian couples families? For that matter, are heterosexual couples families? Or does a couple become a family only when they become parents? Are foster families who care for children for a period of time less a family than adoptive families who make a permanent legal commitment? These issues, outside the scope of this book, are raised to highlight our belief that families need to be viewed in a broad and inclusive context rather than in a narrow, exclusive one.

## The Family as Process

Life is process and family is part of this process. It is not just the emotional and blood bonds that keep families connected. It is the process of spending time together, developing and sharing goals, rituals, and rites of passage that create a family.

It is the process of spending *enough* time together so you can anticipate how others in your family will react to a late dinner, a flat tire, an overdrawn checkbook. You learn to predict with reasonable certainty how birthdays, holidays, and sentimental occasions will be handled. It is this knowledge and its predictability that give individuals a feeling of being part of a family, part of the ongoing and constantly changing process that is the foundation of family.

We must remember that life is not static—it is always in flux, in process. The functions of family and the roles its members play continually shift. And as these shifts take place around us, we struggle as our expectations run to catch up with the reality of new cultural norms about families and our roles as family members.

## The Stepfamily Process

A religious or legal ceremony may create a stepfamily by definition, but it is the process of spending time together developing relationships, sharing tasks, creating a predictability in the ordinary rituals of day-to-day living that build a family unit. Family process, difficult in the "traditional" family, is even more challenging for stepfamilies. Roles for stepfamily members are unclear at best and based on fantasy/folklore prototypes at worst.

This lack of clear role definition creates numerous problems for stepfamily members as they struggle to define themselves and their new family. They often simply do not know what is expected of them or how to act. This is particularly true of the never-married person who marries someone with children.

For stepfamilies, the family process can be arduous and painful. Many people in stepfamilies report that it feels like emotional torture because even when they think they are doing everything right, they may be denied access to acceptance by others who are now labeled as family members. The intensity of the feelings generated are grounded in our need to belong and our beliefs about family as a refuge, a place of emotional security. Until people understand their roles in the family and have some degree of comfort with them, until new family passwords and rituals are developed, family members will not feel accepted, safe, and secure— they will not feel that they belong.

## WHAT IS A STEPFAMILY?

"A stepfamily is a family including a child or children from a previous relationship of one or both parents," is the definition provided by the Stepfamily Association of America, Inc. This broad definition is the one we prefer as it encompasses married couples as well as same-sex and living-together couples. It acknowledges that the dynamics are similar whether or not a couple has legal ties. This definition does not specify where the child or children live. The fact of their existence denotes stepfamily.

Stepfamilies have always been with us, although they are now formed primarily by divorce and remarriage rather than by death and remarriage. This means that a former marriage partner often remains as part of a child's extended family and consequently often remains part of a former mate's life as well.

### Am I a Blended Mother, a Reconstituted Father?

There is a lack of consistency in the professional literature about what to call stepfamilies. We see them referred to as blended families, reconstituted families, REM families, and remarried families. Lay people seem to use the term stepfamily and the corresponding names for individuals in the family, stepmother, stepfather, and stepchild. As a Stepfamily Association of America handout concludes, "a 'blended' mother is an extremely awkward sounding role designation!"

## Different Kinds of Stepfamilies

Researchers who study stepfamilies recognize the need for concise and consistent language that names different kinds of stepfamilies and the people in them. They have delineated three different kinds of stepfamilies, based on who fills the stepparent role. Noting different stepfamily types means that research variables can be more finely drawn, and concise terminology helps clinicians to be more accurate in their descriptions. These terms, as shown in Exhibit 2.1, will be used throughout for consistency.

The term stepfamily does not indicate the primary household where a child lives, because people can be part of a stepfamily and not live together. It also helps to have consistency and clarity in referring to children in stepfamilies.

## BIASES AND PREJUDICES ABOUT STEPFAMILIES

It is now more acceptable to be visible as a stepfamily, to have children from a previous marriage or relationship, to participate in the process of raising someone else's children. Society as a whole is becoming more accepting of stepfamilies, recognizing their complexities and naming the relationships in news broadcasts, television programs, and magazine articles.

This is quite different from the social climate we encountered twenty years ago, when stepfamilies tried to disguise their status, even to the extent of adopting stepchildren so all family members would have the same last name. However, despite their increasing social visibility, stepfamilies continue to be viewed as less acceptable than first-time families. An intact (nuclear) family is the gold standard—all other families don't quite measure up. These biases, as shown in Exhibit 2.2, mean that people in stepfamilies have to work harder to be positive about their family status and their stepfamily roles.

Most of us will continue to struggle with biases that idealize the origi-

---

*Stepfather Families*—husband is a stepfather; only the wife has children from a previous relationship.

*Stepmother Families*—wife is a stepmother; only the husband has children from a previous relationship.

*Complex Stepfamilies*—both husband and wife have children from previous relationships.

*Stepfamily Household*—the household where the children have primary residence.

*Siblings*—children who are biologically related and have the same parents.

*Stepsiblings*—have parents who are married to each other but are not biologically related.

*Half siblings*—children who share one biological parent.

*Mutual Children*—children born to the remarried couple. These children are usually biological half siblings to the other children in the family.

*Residential Stepchildren*—reside most of the time with the remarried couple.

*Nonresidential Stepchildren*—visit the remarried household but do not live there most of the time.

---

**Exhibit 2.1. Stepfamily Terms.**

nal family of mother, father, and their children. This constellation, which is increasingly referred to as "first-marriage families" rather than "nuclear families," is the prized standard against which other families are judged. Yet the fact that they are now so labeled indicates a profound shift in the demographics of most American families.

If you think you don't have biases and prejudices about stepfamilies, think again. Are there any of us who are not conditioned by the stories we hear as children? Did Cinderella have a *good* stepmother who treated her as she treated her own daughters? Did Hansel and Gretel's stepmother take them to Disneyland?

Most of us unconsciously pair the word stepmother with wicked, stepfather with abusive, and stepchild with neglected. These word pairs, or the use of the word stepchild as an adjective meaning neglected, continue to be seen in printed material, perpetuating our cultural biases at a subliminal level and coloring how we all feel about stepfamilies and the kinds of relationships that develop in them.

These biases mean that people in stepfamilies have to work harder to be positive about their family status and their stepfamily roles:

- Stepmothers are wicked.

- Stepfathers are abusive.

- Stepchildren are neglected.

- Stepfamilies aren't real families.

- Stepfamilies aren't as good as first-marriage families.

- Stepfamilies should pretend to be first-marriage families.

**Exhibit 2.2. Cultural Biases and Prejudices About Stepfamilies.**

Why else would Mala, after disciplining her stepdaughter, occasionally ask Roger, "Was that a mean thing to do? I feel like a wicked stepmother when I ask Kira to clean up her room." Where those feelings come from is not as important as recognizing they are there, in one form or another, for all of us. We must be aware of them so that we do not send signals to our clients that stepfamilies are in any way less valuable than other families.

What about television? We are embarrassed to recall that we told our children they would love being in a stepfamily because "It will be just like the Brady Bunch," a TV series popular at the time of our remarriage. In retrospect, we see the Bradys as a stepfamily retrofitted to appear as a first-marriage family, but at the time it was a reassuring presentation as we fantasized erasing prior husbands and wives and living happily ever after.

Probably the most powerful of all influences on our personal biases about stepfamilies are the stories we are told about our own families. When we became a stepfamily and started working with stepfamily clients, we did not recognize that we had stepfamilies in our family lines. We knew that there had been deaths and remarriages, but these remarried families were not called stepfamilies in the stories told at family get-togethers.

Mala's mother grew up in what was always called the "second" family. She was one of five children born to her father's second wife. His first wife died bearing child number six in the "first" family, and a new bride (Mala's grandmother) came shortly thereafter from Norway. Interestingly, the family stories about the first and second families never mentioned that Mala's grandmother was stepmother to her husband's six children. But Mala recalls the stories of the ongoing contention between Bertha, the oldest daughter in the first family, and Malla, the new bride. Only now can we imagine the difficult dynamics and label the relationships properly. Somehow, because the first wife was deceased, Mala never perceived her mother as being part of a stepfamily. In fact, she was a mutual child in a stepfamily household.

Roger knew that his father's mother had died when his father was six. He also knew Aunt Sue was his father's half sister. When Roger questioned his father about his stepmother, saying he had never heard him speak of her, his father's reply was vitriolic. At age 82, he still harbored profound resentment about the fact that she had "replaced" his mother. He was a stepchild raised in a stepmother household. His half sibling was the mutual child of the remarried couple.

We must assume that even though our antecedent families were not labeled as stepfamilies, they colored to some degree our own ways of viewing stepfamilies or our need to make them invisible. Most of us don't have to look too far to find stepfamilies in our own family constellations. And like us, you may have unrecognized stepfamilies closer than you think.

## Clinical Biases and Prejudices

During our professional education, we are inadvertently taught pre judices about families. Our disciplines teach us to hunt for problems, labeling as dysfunctional families exhibiting behaviors that do not meet with our approval or comply with some mythological norm. We are trained to be intrapsychic detectives seeking clues, sniffing out pathology.

Our modus operandi is to hunt for dysfunction and label it, then repair or excise it. A good grounding in stepfamily dynamics and an acceptance of all families is required in order to set aside our usual "pathology detective" mentality and listen compassionately to the pain, confusion, and chaos stepfamilies typically present.

The earliest stepfamily literature, both professional and lay, speaks to the need to change societal views of stepfamilies as aberrant, deficient, even deviant (Einstein, 1982; Visher & Visher, 1980). Clinicians whose goal was to turn stepfamilies into families that felt and interacted like first-marriage families did not understand the realities of adjustment faced by stepfamily members, creating shame and guilt about what have come to be accepted as normal and predictable emotional reactions.

Clinicians who help stepfamilies understand that the feelings they experience are normal for most people in stepfamilies model an important tolerance for differences.

How can clinicians overcome their own biases about stepfamilies not being as good as "normal" families? We all need to be aware of how we conceptualize families, how they operate, who belongs in them, what functions they serve, and so on. Once we are aware of our own internal maps about what it means to be a member of a family, we can see if our beliefs allow including stepfamilies as normative families. If we recognize censure, judgment, or intolerance about different kinds of families, we must rebuild and broaden our definitions until they are inclusive rather than restrictive.

If we believe that first-marriage families are the standard against which all other families are to be measured, we will see stepfamilies, as well as other family forms, as deficiency models. This view bypasses the strengths and resiliency of other family types. If we view first-marriage families as the standard, we may make assumptions about how marriage can solve the deficiencies of single-parent families. This bias pushes stepfamilies to be invisible and disappear. To work successfully with stepfamilies, clinicians must have enough knowledge about how they differ from first-marriage families to validate these differences rather than view them as pathological. (See Exhibit 2.3.)

## CLINICIANS' REACTIONS TO STEPFAMILY CLIENTS

It is the intense emotional reactions to stepfamily adjustment that confuse clinicians unfamiliar with how it feels to be in a stepfamily, particularly in the early stages of adjustment. There is so much information to be gathered, and the presentation of that information, the intensity of the couple's feelings, may make the therapist uneasy. The clinician is faced with experiencing the overwhelming quality of the family. But when you know about stepfamily dynamics, this chaos becomes understandable and predictable.

If a therapist does not assume that the family reactions he or she is seeing are normal, it is easy to diagnose a borderline personality, a neurotic process, or character disorders. In fact, we view mild reactive depression and anxiety as normal reactions to how out-of-control stepfamilies often feel. We often comment to people in treatment that we would be more concerned if they weren't reporting feeling depressed and anxious and overwhelmed.

- Stepfamilies are a deviant family form.
- First-marriage families are the "gold standard."
- Remarriage solves postdivorce problems.
- Stepfamilies operate just like first-marriage families.
- Relationships in stepfamilies should be like those in first-marriage families.

**Exhibit 2.3. Clinical Biases and Prejudices About Stepfamilies.**

The clinician's acknowledgment of his or her own sense of being overwhelmed and confused about the new family can validate the experience of family members. The underlying message is that it is necessary to learn to tolerate this current discomfort, which will improve with time.

## SUMMARY: NORMALIZE THE PROCESS

As clinicians we are often uncomfortable with the process of change. We often want quick fixes as much as the families who come to us want them. The underlying message we must give our stepfamily clients is that what they are experiencing is the normal process of becoming a stepfamily. The single most effective strategy we can use to assist our clients in tolerating the discomfort of the stepfamily process is to normalize it.

# CHAPTER 3

# *Developmental Processes*

The stepfamily clinician must be aware of the family, marital, and individual (both adult and children) developmental processes, which proceed interactively. Stepfamily developmental stages occur simultaneously, but often incongruently, with other individual and marital developmental processes (Papernow, 1994). If too much energy is being funneled into stepfamily adjustments, there may not be enough energy left for other developmental tasks, or vice versa. In our brief-therapy model, our goal is not to provide detailed education about other developmental models but to create a contextual viewpoint of couples and other family members simultaneously in a number of different developmental sequences.

## ASSUMPTION #2: DEVELOPMENTAL PROCESSES DRIVE STEPFAMILY ADJUSTMENT.

The key words to remember in thinking about developmental changes and stress in stepfamilies are *multiple and lengthy.* So many things are changing and being rearranged at one time, it is no wonder people are confused and overwhelmed. People don't know where to start to begin to make order out of the chaos they are experiencing. Helping couples and family members identify developmental issues of all kinds helps them to understand where they are in the process and can give them a sense of movement when they feel overwhelmed and stuck. (See Exhibit 3.1.)

It isn't that people in stepfamilies, as a whole, are less able to cope with change and stress; it is that the stressors are multiple and, because of the long adjustment period, seem to be unremitting. People who undergo repeated stress often lose their resiliency, their ability to re-

Identifying developmental issues helps clients:

- Highlight normalcy
- Define issues
- Clarify issues in each area
- Highlight and order discrete problems for solution
- Demarcate their positions
- Understand the potential for overload
- Gain perspective on how they are doing

**Exhibit 3.1. Identifying Developmental Issues.**

group and forge ahead. The new marriage is going through its own adjustment period at the same time that all the family members are each making adjustments to the multiple changes such as where the family lives, lifestyles, new rules, new roles, and so on. And many families are confronted during the early years with still unresolved issues with former spouses that may be costly emotionally and financially if the battle moves into the legal arena.

Additionally, there is the burden of trying to figure out what to fix first. Adults often focus on children's issues, but often they are in enough emotional pain themselves that they are effectively unavailable to the children. Children's emotional needs must be considered and balanced with the needs of the new and still fragile couple relationship.

The developmental needs of the individuals in the new family are frequently out of step (and may be at odds) with the adults' need to make the family "feel like family" as quickly as possible. For example, adolescents who are on the verge of leaving the family unit may not be as receptive to family activities as younger children. The life-cycle issues that confront adults also may be incongruent. The man in his late forties who has almost finished raising his children and has recently married a younger, childless woman who wants to start a family would be a classic example.

It is also important to note temperamental differences, which mean that some adults and children cope with change and its concomitant stress better than others. For example, we operate on the assumption that most children are relatively flexible and can handle a fair amount of change if they are supported and given information about the process. Some children, however, do not tolerate change well at all. The emotional temperament of these children needs to be taken into consideration.

Adults have temperamental differences as well. Part of the adjustment for stepfamilies is learning about and learning to live with everyone else's quirks. It is not unlike one corporation combining with another. During the reorganization, there is a period of confusion, upset, concurrent stress, and jockeying for position before the new corporation's management and employees have a sense of the new corporate identity.

Many of the changes and stresses that stepfamilies go through are expected and predictable. It helps people in stepfamilies to feel more in control if they have an idea of what may come up and are given tips on how to handle common situations. Subjects in Papernow's (1994) research sample, which studied stepfamily developmental stages, did not connect their family struggles with the "normal developmental process of becoming a stepfamily" (p. 7). Rather, they tended to regard themselves "as members of poorly functioning biological families" (p. 7). Papernow also notes that this perspective seemed common among helping professionals.

## THE STEPFAMILY CYCLE—A PROCESS CONTINUUM

We first started hearing of Patricia Papernow's work on a developmental cycle for stepfamilies in 1980. We called her in Boston, and she graciously sent us a copy of her Ph.D. thesis, which we read with great interest. It clarified some issues we had been seeing in our new stepfamily-focused practice and confirmed some ideas we had about interventions we were finding useful. (It was this early work that was the basis for her 1994 book, *Becoming a Stepfamily*.)

Papernow's developmental framework is an important part of the knowledge foundation stepfamily clinicians need. Like all developmental theory, stages do not always proceed in an exact linear fashion, nor can we predict with accuracy how long any given family or individual will spend in each stage. We corroborate her belief that individual members of a stepfamily may be in different stages at the same time.

The articulation of a developmental process is enormously helpful because it provides context by placing people in a process along a continuum, which by its very nature is not static. Papernow's stepfamily cycle also overlays individual development on family system development, creating a useful multidimensional perspective.

The power of the stepfamily cycle is that it places different adjustments in the context of normal development. "As long as normal stepfamily dynamics remain unfamiliar," Papernow (1994) indicates, "people will [not] be adequately assisted with a central dilemma of their lives: the complicated process of making safe, reliable, nourishing relationships in a stepfamily" (p. 7).

Her research indicates that it takes four to seven years for a stepfamily to move through the necessary stages of development. It is neither feasible nor appropriate to have couples or families in treatment for such a protracted period of time. To do so diminishes and denigrates their efforts and coping abilities. Thus, the Step By Step Model uses a series of focused interventions that respond to the needs of the family at any particular point, helping them overcome the obstacles to moving through the developmental sequence.

## Point of View

Papernow's model "presents a developmental model built from the viewpoint of stepfamily members" (p. 10). This is unlike such theoretical models as family systems theory, which often describes the life cycle from the outside perspective of the helping professional looking in at family functioning. When a clinician adopts Papernow's model the clinician is enabled to join with a stepfamily in a way that otherwise would be difficult. It creates a climate of collaboration between clinician and client that plays to clients' strengths and does not impose a power hierarchy between client and clinician.

The stepfamily cycle is the "process by which boundaries (individual, intergenerational, couple, interfamilial) move from biological to 'step'" (p. 12). Papernow continues, "My data clearly indicates that speed and ease of movement through the Stepfamily Cycle are often closely related to the amount and timing of support, particularly in the early stages. Support is defined as the presence of someone or something that provides validation for and understanding of intense painful feelings involved in early stepfamily living, and some indication of what to do next" (p. 18).

## Papernow's Stepfamily Cycle

Although Papernow divides the early, middle, and late stages of her stepfamily cycle into subdivisions, for the sake of simplicity we will look at each of these stages as a continuum of experience, recognition, and awareness gained as individuals move toward the next stage.

Papernow notes that her data "indicates that children may move at a very different developmental pace and rhythm through the Stepfamily Cycle than adults" (p. 69) and so "it is crucial to note that children and adults in the same family may actually be at different stages at any one point in their family history" (p. 69).

## THE STEPFAMILY CYCLE: THE STAGES

The three stages of the stepfamily cycle—early, middle, and later—are listed in Exhibit 3.2.

### The Early Stages: Fantasy, Immersion, and Awareness

The challenges of the early stage of this developmental framework involve recognition not only of the fantasies held by family members about who will play what role and how these roles will be enacted, but also of the beliefs, usually deeply held, about what wounds and past hurts will be healed in these new relationships. On the continuum, this involves being immersed in the reality of stepfamily life so that expectations and beliefs about a family member's fantasies are tested by the realities of current experience.

*Early Stages*
Fantasy
Immersion
Awareness

*Middle Stages*
Mobilization
Action

*Later Stages*
Contact
Resolution

**Exhibit 3.2. The Stages of the Stepfamily Cycle.**

I was really looking forward to our first family vacation. It was supposed to be fun, a time for everybody in the family to get to know
each other. So far, Eric's only spoken to me once—to tell me my car
sucked—and you and I have done nothing but fight.

—Stepfather of a 10-year-old boy, in a remarriage of one year

Recognition of the multiple differences of experience in the family is
the hallmark of this part of the early stages. What roles are being played
out and how, who feels part of the family and who feels like an outsider,
the tugs on the biological parent that create distance in the developing
couple bond, all serve as unsettling reminders that this is not what family members thought it was going to be. To move forward on the continuum, individuals must begin to verbalize their increasing awareness
of how it really feels to be part of this developing family and the expectations and fantasies that are being shattered.

I always thought if I had little girls I would make velveteen dresses for
them to wear at Christmas. Now I've got two adorable stepdaughters,
it's our year for Christmas visitation, I made the dresses as a surprise,
and they cried because they wanted to wear the K-Mart dresses their
mother sent with them.

—New stepmother of nonresidential stepdaughters, ages 5 and 7

Those who work with stepfamilies must not underestimate the intrapsychic pain and grief an individual must go through in order to relinquish tenaciously held fantasies. Our experience as clinicians and
stepfamily members is that letting go of the pain of unrealistic expectations may be an unrealistic expectation. An individual's recognition of
the feelings and their source, along with appropriate management of
his or her response, may be a more reasonable goal. This caveat stems
from our 20 years in a stepfamily and the sometimes surprising feelings
of sadness that arise, particularly around life-passage events.

The growing awareness of the realities of stepfamily living, which
Papernow (1994) refers to as creating "a more accurate map of the
[stepfamily] territory" (p. 382), and verbalization of feelings establish a
climate in which family members can ask each other, "What does it feel
like for you?." Empathy about another's reality becomes more possible
when our feelings are soothed by the dawning recognition and acceptance
of how living in a stepfamily differs from life in a first-marriage family.

Papernow asserts that some families begin here, towards the end of
the continuum of the early stages, bypassing the earlier phases of that

stage. She also indicates that many families get stuck in the middle of the early stages, immersed in the reality of stepfamily living and unable to begin to make sense of it.

> I thought by our first wedding anniversary we'd be a real family. We've been married for two and a half years and I can't seem to make anybody happy. What are we doing wrong?
>
> —Stepfather of stepdaughter, age 8, and stepson, age 10

## The Middle Stages: Mobilization and Action

It continues to be helpful to conceptualize progress in the stepfamily cycle as movement on a continuum. During the middle stages, the family begins to mobilize to work together more effectively as what Papernow calls the "biological force fields" around the biological subsystems in the family begin to break down. This difficult transition is often facilitated by an outpouring of frustration of a stepparent attempting to exert more influence on how the family runs.

It is during this period that the biological parent may feel intense loyalty conflicts while the stepparent actively advocates for more participation in the family, trying to clarify what role each will play.

> You and Michael always make these plans for the weekend and somehow I never seem to get included unless I make a stink about it. And if I go along I feel like a fifth wheel. Am I a part of this family or not?
>
> —Stepmother of stepson, age 11, in a three-year marriage

While experienced as a shaky time in most stepfamilies, this unsettled period is a necessary precursor to system changes, which must occur for the family to move forward as a stepfamily. Action directed toward mutually agreed-upon goals helps to clarify family roles and strengthen dyadic relationships.

Papernow frequently uses the adjectives "nourishing" and "reliable" to describe the types of stepfamily relationships that need to be developed, and she speaks to the need to develop workable stepparent roles. Interactions in the stepfamily, toward the end of the middle stages, are beginning to feel predictable.

> Did you notice that? He actually brought his math homework to me so I could help him.
>
> —Stepfather of stepson, age 12, in a 4-year-old remarriage

Don't forget that individuals may be at different places on the continuum at different times. It is not unusual to see a couple where the stepparent is rocking the boat in the middle stages and a biological parent is holding tenaciously to the fantasies of the early stages.

## The Later Stages: Contact and Resolution

The later stages of stepfamily development are marked by contacts that feel more comfortable and satisfying and by emerging feelings of resolution in these contacts. For the most part, stepparents know the roles they play in the family. Relationships among individuals have evolved so there is predictability about how they interact and the kinds of relationships they have. The family has evolved reliable ways of working together and family rituals have developed, creating a sense of family permanence. Stepfamily issues, as such, are rarely the focus of attention in these later stages.

For children, the reliable knowledge of secure membership in multiple households and relationships means that they can move forward with their own developmental tasks. Papernow (1994) cautions that life-passage events may resurrect the pain of being an outsider in a stepfamily and "offer...opportunities to rework divorce, death and loyalty conflicts" (p. 386).

When we see later stages stepfamilies in our offices, it is frequently around these sorts of issues or adult reactions to an adult child who is stuck developmentally in an earlier stage.

> John is 24 and still lives with us. He moved in after he dropped out of college four years ago and is waiting tables. At first I was really glad to have him with us—I missed so much of his growing up years. But, he can't seem to get himself mobilized. I guess we're afraid he'll still be in the family room five years from now. We're ready to be alone.
>
> —Biological father and his wife of 12 years

## Time Frame of the Stepfamily Cycle

This developmental continuum provides an important perspective on the nature of the adjustments stepfamilies go through and the extended period of time involved, usually four to seven years. Papernow (1994) indicates that "stepfamilies tend to 'make it or break it' by the fourth year" (p. 18) and reports that the families who make the necessary transitions and adjustments most easily are the "families [who come] to stepfamily living with fewer deeply held fantasies and more realistic expectations" (p. 19). She indicates that *average* families are able to navigate the cycle in seven years.

In our clinical practice, where most families have been self-referred, we frequently see families at the end of the early stages or at some point during the middle stages. In a sample of 179 families seen in our practice between 1979 and 1989, 77.6 percent were couples who had been married less than four years.

## Summary of Papernow's Contribution

The power of normalizing developmental stages as part of the context of the adjustments stepfamilies go through cannot be overemphasized. To know that most people in stepfamilies experience similar feelings, frustrations, and confusion is validating and healing. This piece of education for stepfamilies ought to be part of any intervention where clients are in a stepfamily (even if stepfamily issues are not the reason for the intervention). For stepfamily clinicians, it is the process orientation of the stepfamily cycle that is conceptually vital.

## MARITAL/FAMILY DEVELOPMENT

Remarriages must be viewed from multiple developmental contexts, and we utilize our own schema for placing a remarried couple on a continuum of marital/family development. This schema includes some of Kimmel's (1974) Family Stages, to which we have added *planning on marriage* and *living together*. The stages in our schema are those most frequently seen in our client population. As with other developmental frameworks, the stages are not necessarily discrete and sometimes they overlap. Our commentary about these stages focuses on the impact of being in a stepfamily. (See Exhibit 3.3.)

## Planning on Marriage

The planning stage does not exist at all for those impulsive individuals who remarry. Planning is also often lacking in perfectly well-functioning

- Planning on Marriage
- Living Together
- First Year (Living Together or Marriage)
- Child Rearing (Prior to Adolescence)
- Child Departure Mode (Adolescence)
- Post-Child Adjustment

**Exhibit 3.3. Marital Development Stages.**

people who do other things reasonably well. We think that this has to do with massive denial and the unrealistic expectation that stepfamilies "blend" on their own. The smartest couples are those who inform themselves, heed the warnings, and work hard to achieve a reasonable perspective.

Couples who decide not to live together prior to a remarriage may or may not be actively planning to bring their respective families together. They may already understand that the children will not adapt as easily as they hope and they may be paying attention to warning signals. They may also have their heads in the sand or in the clouds. Dedication and the desire for things to go right usually are not enough.

> I saw the grief my sister went through when she remarried. She and Tony just got destroyed by all the problems. That's not going to happen to us.
>
> —27-year-old father of two, planning to remarry in 4 months

## Living Together

Living together, as a stage, sometimes precedes the planning stage. Sometimes living together is a matter of convenience; sometimes it is a matter of a public commitment while a couple waits for a divorce or property settlement. Whether it will show the couple what problems they are facing or those that may come later cannot be predicted.

Reactions of children to a living-together situation vary. Some children hold tight to their fantasy of the biological parents reuniting, and therefore they do not see the living together as indicative of the future. If they have seen their parents separate and reunite several times, they will be unimpressed by the new relationship. If they have been through several "boyfriends" or "girlfriends," this may be perceived as yet another short-term event.

Regardless of children's reactions, most couples face the same kinds of issues when moving in together that they do when a formal remarriage takes place. We consider couples who are living together, when children are involved, to be stepfamilies facing the same problems married stepfamilies confront.

> We can't get married until Rafe's divorce is final, so he moved in with us. Mostly, the kids ignore him, but they tell me we did just fine before he came along. I think they wish he'd go away, but where would that leave me?
>
> —37-year-old single mother of three teenage children

## First Year

The "first year" is a process, not a time—an emotional transition to being a couple. In the first year, the couple learns to live with each other, exploring and learning about the person to whom they have committed. The "first year" can occur whether the couple are married or not. Does this couple have the time to experience the normal development of their relationship? The primary emphasis is on adjusting to an adult relationship, learning how to share physical and emotional space. In the stepfamily, space and time are, of necessity, shared commodities, and this reality can hinder a couple's first-year development.

It may be difficult to identify when the first year occurred or whether, in fact, it has been experienced. Sometimes, other time-consuming and emotional events put the first year adjustment on hold. A prolonged and serious illness of a child or adult may prevent the necessary relationship adjustments, or a lengthy custody battle may take all of a couple's time and financial resources. Couples tell us that often the little shared time they have is spent discussing attorneys and legal events rather than getting to know one another. Only when the legal issues are resolved do they have time to devote to their relationship.

> We hadn't been married for three months when Jane's ex-husband sued for custody. It's finally settled after two years, but we've got a pile of debt it will take years to pay off and we can hardly remember why we got married in the first place.
>
> —42-year-old, remarried for three years

## Child Rearing

In the first family, months are spent anticipating the beginning of the parenting years. In a stepfamily, there may be little time for anticipating or preparing, while unrealistic expectations often foster a belief that little preparation is needed. People may find themselves thrust into a child-rearing role, and the number of children involved may vary as a result of shifts in visitation. There is usually a strong focus on the children as part of the household. The first-year adjustment of the couple occurs simultaneously with children's developmental needs and is, unfortunately, often relegated to the back burner as more pressing child issues take precedence.

> Even though I don't have kids of my own, I've been a pediatric nurse for six years, so taking care of Jerry's little boy on the weekends should have been easy. Let me tell you, this stepmother thing is the hardest thing I've ever done.
>
> —Stepmother of 4-year-old stepson

Most couples have a perception of working toward being a family of sorts, with the expectation that eventually the family will form a workable unit. However, they are often unrealistic about the variety of family resolutions possible for stepfamilies.

## Departure Mode for Adolescents

Referring to adolescents as being in "departure mode" is a useful way for people in stepfamilies to look at these children. Parenting, including structure and guidance, is still very much needed. However, while the adults' orientation may be toward consolidation and forming a family, older adolescents are clearly in a developmental stage that requires them to disengage as they prepare to leave the family home.

Integrating into the new family runs against the profound pull of the developmental task of preparing to leave the family. When the parents can clearly view the adolescents as being oriented outward, preparing to start their own lives as independent adults, it is remarkable to see how the adults can relax and adjust their expectations.

Parents have very different feelings than stepparents during this stage. A parent may be emotionally pulled in a more profound way as a biological child prepares to leave. It may resurrect guilt from the divorce period or fear of yet another emotional loss even when the parent views a child's departure with pride, an acknowledgment of good parenting.

A stepparent may also view the departure with mixed feelings: ambivalence about a possibly unfinished relationship with a stepchild, and relief and anticipation of increased time to spend with a spouse. For other couples, the prospect of being alone for the first time, after years of exhausting family struggle, is frightening.

> My preference would be for Emily to go to school at least 3000 miles away. Frank wants her home attending community college. Of course, Emily and I have butted heads a lot since her dad and I got married and I think Frank's still devastated by all he missed because of the divorce.
>
> —48-year-old stepmother of a stepdaughter, age eighteen

## Post-Child Adjustment

If a couple comes for consultation after the children are grown and have left home, they may not be coming about stepfamily matters, but that issue gives them permission to seek assistance. They may be struggling with life-passage events, wills, or inheritance decisions, issues that are more complicated for stepfamilies. It is also possible that they are not really in the post-child adjustment phase. Emotional adolescence does not end with a birthday and that same birthday is no guarantee of responsible mature behavior by young adults. Children do not necessarily leave home all at once or permanently, and many adult children find themselves back at home for a variety of reasons.

Having an adult child or stepchild creates a series of problematic issues. Couples may be confronted with dependent children living at home or coming home more often than the parents would like. A child's unrecognized, mild depression, born of a failure to resolve a divorce and remarriage during earlier years, may be at issue. Sometimes, dependent young adults need attention and direction to begin their lives, along with a gentle, structured push out of the nest.

House rules become an issue when adult children live at home. Young adults expects to come and go as they please and may not recognize the need for the courtesy of informing parents where they are and when they will return home. Parents may have been looking forward to more order in their households and may have to assert their needs.

> I don't get it. I'm 23 and they're still trying to tell me what to do. My
> stepfather got on my case this morning when he heard me come in at
> 2:30 A.M. I tried to keep quiet. Can I help it if he's a light sleeper?
>
> —23-year-old stepchild

Remarriages that take place well after children have grown and left
home may set off considerable problems with adult children. They may
fail to welcome the new stepparent, treat him or her as a stranger and
outsider in "their" home, or do things such as coming in to remove some
of "Mom's" furniture to which they feel entitled.

Although the children are "gone," the couple may need counseling
concerning how to respond, assert themselves, and set boundaries about
territory and behavior. Because these children will never live at home,
the opportunity to develop relationships is less available and the family
history to be overcome by a stepparent means that insider/outsider issues
will be paramount. Grandparent issues may also surface when stepgrand-
parents may be reminded of not being blood relatives, even in some
instances when they have participated in raising their stepchildren.

## INDIVIDUAL DEVELOPMENT

Remarriage often reshapes the form of an individual's adult life. Roles
we thought we were finished with—for example, being a parent of a
preschool child—may be revisited. Or we may be catapulted at a younger
than usual age into stepgrandparenthood. Order and symmetry are not
givens in adult life. Emotional work that we assumed would come at a
given time or after another stage can occur out of order and all at once.
Old issues may be reopened as we respond to the changes remarriage
brings to our lives.

We lack a truly comprehensive system to organize the complex process of adult development. Erikson's lifelong developmental model includes adult stages, but most other discussions of adult life focus on
issues of the roles we play in marriage, family, and the workplace. What
adults experience is much more complex than their roles and includes
not just their own reactions to their own history but also the historical
era in which they find themselves.

We think adults often forget that they undergo developmental stages
just as children do. Adults may be establishing or changing careers, adding or ending roles in their new family, or looking forward to time as a

couple. All of these changes require adjustments in many areas of an individual's life.

Perhaps the best compilation of these issues is seen in *Passages* by Gail Sheehy (1984). We consider this useful reading for anyone in a stepfamily, because it helps people to understand the context of the life events they are going through simultaneously with their stepfamily adjustment. Any tools that help order the chaos stepfamily members experience is useful.

Let's look at some of the ways in which being in a stepfamily can reshape an adult's life.

### Acquiring an Adolescent

First families proceed in an orderly development and get to know each other gradually, in expected ways. It can be difficult to suddenly acquire, through marriage, an adolescent, complete with his or her own personality and distinct family history, at a trying developmental stage. The impulse of the adults is to work toward more family integration, but the member of the household in departure mode may not want to be a part of any family, even the old family.

### Becoming a Parent

In most first-marriage families, there are months of positive anticipation and then the arrival of a newborn. Upon remarriage many people become parents for the first time, and usually not of an infant. Suddenly, stepparents acquire one or more children in different developmental stages, although they may have had no experience whatsoever relating to children in a parental role.

### Needing a Job

Becoming part of a stepfamily is a package deal, and the needs of the new family become the obligation of the stepparent. There are often strained financial resources. A stepparent may be required to get a job to help finance the new family, or someone already employed may need to get a second job. Establishing a career for oneself is one thing; having to get a job to support your stepchildren is quite another.

## Facing a Career Plateau

There can be circumstances in which one of the adults faces a career plateau just at the point of remarriage, simultaneously facing a crisis of confidence and uncertainty about the vocational future at work and at the same time trying to come to terms with a new identity defined by relationships with the new people in his or her life.

## Couple's Intimacy

Getting close in the context of the multiple adjustments faced because one is part of a stepfamily can be logistically difficult as well as emotionally frightening. It may be the reality of being emotionally intimate for the first time that is at issue, or there may have been a difficult or loveless prior marriage that raises anxiety about new and intimate emotional relationships. There are many scenarios that reflect the fears associated with intimacy in remarriage.

## Sharing Independence

Both parties to the marriage may have issues about independence and what it means to share the work and handle the needs of the family. However, it is most likely that the larger issue may be that of the woman who has had a period in her life when she was totally independent. The independence issue may be something that people assume occurs at the threshold of adulthood, but for some women it may be deferred for a very long time and become an issue in remarriage.

## CHILDHOOD DEVELOPMENT

There is a large body of knowledge about the development of children. This literature is quite complex and clearly beyond the scope of this book. We make the assumption that as mental health professionals our readers will have a grasp of the issues that arise as children pass through the various physical, emotional, and psychosocial stages in their lives.

Because we use a couple's model, we usually do not see the children in our sessions. However, the couples we see are concerned about their children; in fact, concern about a child often precipitates the first phone contact with us. Providing parents with appropriate developmental information can assuage their fears about how their children are coping with remarriage. We provide parents with a reading list and may suggest other parenting resources, such as parenting classes or video and audiotapes.

As clinicians, we have our own memories and experiences as parents to bring to bear on the child-focused problems brought to us by the families we work with. Clinicians who are not parents can share what they have learned about normal childhood developmental stages. It is helpful to couples seeking our consultation to be provided with information about what is normally expected from children at various ages. This is particularly true for stepparents who have no parenting experience.

The issue for couples who consult with us is the need to separate problem behavior from normal behavior. There is a tendency to view all problematic behavior and emotional reactions as caused by the disruption of the first marriage and the subsequent remarriage.

We expect children to react, and parents need to understand that children's reactions are going on at the same time that children are going through their own developmental passages. This makes more complex the task of sorting out problem behavior from behavior we view as predictable and expected reactions to a remarriage.

We view most parents as capable of learning to assist their children through reactions even to difficult life transitions. We may suggest strategies for helping a child through an adjustment and then taking some time to see if the problem will resolve itself. A time frame is set for parents to get in touch with us again if the behavior has not improved, further evaluation may be needed at that point. With information, parents can learn to sort out adjustment issues inherent in their family from issues that appear in all children. At times, children need more help than parents can provide. Assessment and referral will be discussed in Chapter 9, Vulnerability.

## SUMMARY

We began this chapter by using the adjectives multiple and lengthy to describe the kinds of developmental adjustments faced by stepfamilies. Layering the stepfamily cycle over the multiple life-cycle adjustments increases the overwhelming quality of life experienced by many stepfamilies. Our belief is that understanding and education about these developmental processes will reduce the sense of helplessness many people in stepfamilies experience.

Our job as clinicians is to educate and clarify for the couple what to expect from their children and themselves in these various developmental stages, point out areas of congruence and potential incongruence, and alert them to how stepfamily development interacts with other life-cycle passages.

# CHAPTER 4

# *Structure*

The concept of structure in the Step By Step model is comprised of four elements: composition, time frames, mechanics, and relationship hot spots. This chapter provides an overview of these elements, normal parts of the stepfamily context and process, which reliably predict treatment issues and interventions for stepfamilies.

Structural information, gained in the Stepfamily Assessment sessions (Chapter 7), is the snapshot in time that allows the clinician to hypothesize about family interactions. Knowledge about the dynamics of stepfamilies and how they differ from first-marriage families is the theoretical base for generating these hypotheses.

## ASSUMPTION #3: THE STRUCTURE OF THE STEPFAMILY PREDICTS ISSUES THAT WILL BE A FOCUS OF TREATMENT.

It is not just who resides in a household (the most basic structural element). It is the relationships between family members that speak to clinical issues—who is in the family, physically and emotionally, and who is out. Stepfamilies are complex systems of individuals in multiple layers of relationships. By looking at how the relationship systems are affected by structure we can predict problematic areas of functioning in the whole system.

There is inevitable overlap among the four elements of structure. For example, while visitation is primarily a mechanical piece, its effects are more than just logistical. And don't forget that the term stepfamily does not designate the primary household where a child lives. People can be part of a stepfamily and not live together; however, considering both where children reside and visitation issues can assist the clinician in predicting potential problem areas for both residential and nonresidential stepfamilies.

## COMPOSITION

Composition tells us about who the members of this family are, who lives in this household, and who visits. One of the reasons stepfamilies are complicated is that family members are part of overlapping family systems. The overlap creates continually shifting physical and emotional boundaries around family subsystems.

For example, the newly married couple planning a "family" get together is not likely to include former spouses, yet those former spouses are family members to the children involved. Early in our marriage, we planned a party for the Labor Day weekend. Mala's eight-year-old son, Ted, asked, "Is Dad coming?" "No," Mala replied, "this is a party for just the family." "But Dad is part of *my* family," was Ted's confused response, a response that spoke eloquently to the different family configurations that must coexist.

Children must be given access to biological parents and the extended families of nonresidential parents. Yet this access often feels against the grain, a violation of the new couple's need to pull tight the boundaries that define the new unit as family. And until the couple has more history, until the members are more comfortable with their sense of the new family as a stable unit with predictable rhythms and a shared history to recall, they often remain rigid about access issues. The composition of the family remains unclear for quite some time as the subsystems in the family, reminders of current alliances and previous history, polarize insider/outsider dilemmas. The subheads in this section reflect the kinds of issues related to the composition of the stepfamily.

## Number of Children

It is difficult enough to help one child through the stepfamily adjustment, but it is exponentially more complicated if there are multiple children, each with his or her own history and reaction to the previous marital disruption and the subsequent changes. Who is in the household at any given time and the differences between how the household operates then and at other times may become foci of intervention.

## Developmental Stages of the Children

If there is more than one child in the stepfamily, there is the potential for a wide range of developmental stages, potentially bewildering to the couple and necessitating attention to very different concerns. Having multiple adolescents will be particularly difficult. Younger children, who have shorter family histories, may be less resistant to being assimilated into the new family.

The clinician can put together a picture for the couple of the issues they will be facing. A particular child's functioning may be at issue, but even when the children are not presented as the primary concern, the clinician needs to assist the couple with awareness of children's adjustment issues.

## Where Do the Children Live?

If the children live with the mother and stepfather, there is more time for relationships to be formed simply because of physical proximity. However, the couple may be forced to deal with negotiating discipline issues and addressing authority issues in the household earlier than if the children lived with the other parent. Accepted wisdom among stepfamily experts is that discipline should be mutually agreed upon by the couple, but should initially be pronounced and enforced by the biological parent. This is especially helpful in stepfamilies with children who have not yet reached adolescence. The biological parent must empower the stepparent with statements such as, "John's going to be in charge while I'm at the store."

If children are adolescents, more authoritative (as opposed to authoritarian) parenting has been found to foster the development of better relationships between the stepparent and stepchild. Authoritative parenting was characterized by "higher levels of positivity and monitoring, moderate to high levels of control, and low negativity (Heatherington & Clingempeel, 1992). Sensitive implementation of house rules is essential, but this does not mean that expectations for behavior are not monitored and enforced. Clinicians may need to help parents and stepparents understand that the parental hierarchy is multifaceted and not just about rules and their enforcement.

## Why Do Children Reside Where They Do ?

Following their parents' divorce the majority of children live with their mother. In Maryland, where our practice is located, many divorced couples have joint custody, but in most cases the children's primary residence is with their mother. Over time there are often informal changes of residence, but these changes are not necessarily preceded or followed by legal changes in custody.

If a father starts out with custody of the children, it is important to know why. The reasons are usually important and informative. Occasionally, couples tell us that the decision to have children reside with the father was well thought out and jointly agreed upon by both biological parents because it addressed the best interests of the children. Much more often we find other reasons why the custody situation is atypical—reasons that almost always affect the development of the new family and the emotional adjustment of the children.

## Does the Stepfather Have Biological Children Elsewhere?

This can be an issue that poses difficulties in terms of family composition, mechanics, and relationship hot spots. Stepfathers who do not live with their biological children often express tremendous pain at not being with their kids full time. Sometimes, stepfathers handle this sadness matter-of-factly; many more are not aware of their upset, which can create distance and tension in their relationships with their stepchildren.

How are the stepfather's children incorporated into the new household? Is this a disruption or have entry and exit rituals been established? You will want to know how a father stays in touch with his children between visits and whether this contact creates any problems in the marital relationship.

## Mutual Child

In our practice, we occasionally see couples who have a mutual child, but issues around these children are rarely the focus of intervention.

For a complete study of this issue, we recommend *Yours, Mine, and Ours* by Anne Bernstein (1989), who believes that the mutual child can provide important connections for nonbiologically related family members (stepsiblings acquire a half sibling biologically related to both sides of the family) and may serve to strengthen a couple's resolve to work through difficult marital periods.

Some of our client families with a mutual child born much later than the children of the first families have reported that this new family feels like another first-marriage family. They anecdotally report that this mutual child allowed them to parent in a way they were not able to before, in effect giving them a second chance at parenthood. Bernstein's interviews (1989) with couples that have a mutual child supported this common theme.

More frequently, we see couples who are trying to decide whether to have a child together. This can be a major stumbling block, even for couples who had discussed this issue prior to their marriage and decided not to have children together. Many times couples, where the man had children and the woman did not, have sought help when the woman who had thought that she could be happy without having a child, changed her mind as she reached her middle thirties. Her husband may have felt betrayed as a previous agreement is reopened for discussion. He may have been seeing the light at the end of the child-rearing tunnel while she longed for maternal fulfillment.

In our experience, this issue frequently seems to arise at a time when a man is burdened with college expenses for the children from his previous marriage. But the biological imperative to reproduce often takes on a life of its own and creates relationship issues for the couple that are not connected to relationship issues between stepparent and stepchild.

At times the issue is fertility. He has had a vasectomy after having his children and she may want him to attempt a reversal. Or they may agree on having a child, but be unable to conceive. In a number of cases where the wife did not have children, a husband's willingness to attempt a vasectomy reversal or undergo fertility testing was enough commitment to allow the partner to let go of the dream of becoming a parent.

## Composition Summary

Composition—who is in the household at any given time—raises multiple areas of potential adjustment difficulties that may need to be addressed. There is an inevitable overlap of composition with the mechanical issues of how children move between the two households. Research literature is beginning to offer useful information about stepparenting roles with children of different ages.

## TIME FRAMES

Time frames refer to when composition changes occur in families and their duration. For example, important time frames for stepfamilies include the time between a marital separation and a remarriage and either the single-parent phase or the time a person spends as a childless single adult. Information about these periods says a great deal about the kind of adjustments being faced by the people in this stepfamily. Remember that individuals in a family will perceive events in different ways. A child will perceive the first day of a separation as the end of the marriage; the adults are more likely to view the day their divorce is granted legally as the end of the marriage. We must help adults understand the cognitive limitations their children have when trying to make sense of changes in the household.

If we could design an ideal set of circumstances, we might choose to allow the adults and children two to three years between separation and the remarriage to adjust to the divorce. The single-parent phase would be time limited; after it is completed, the next phase, remarriage, could be embarked upon. But the world rarely works that way. Sometimes remarriage comes close on the heels of separation and divorce or death; sometimes it comes many years later. The following subheads indicate a variety of time frame issues we have seen in our client families.

### Multiple Separations

Parents may separate a number of times. Each separation is difficult for the adults, but it is especially hard on the children, who often do not have the cognitive abilities to understand what is happening. It also sets them up for unreasonable hopes of reconciliation after a final separation takes place. If this has occurred, children may be unable to overcome their hopes of parental reunion in order to allow themselves to develop a relationship with a stepparent.

We view sequential living together situations as setting up the same emotional scenario for children. Why should they invest in a relationship with yet another "significant other"? Why should they trust that this new relationship will last any longer than the other one had? Again, the adult's perspective will be quite different from the children's. Clinicians can help the adults put the children's predictable responses into a perspective that includes the child's point of view.

### Single-Parent Phase

When there is just one parent in the household, the parent–child relationship often becomes closer and more intense. These relationships have implications for the children's as well as the adult's adjustment to a remarriage. Most children live with their mothers after divorce, and we do not view some level of enmeshment between a single mother and her children as pathological. This tight alliance is understandable because of time spent in a single-parent household.

However, there will be predictable issues of inclusion for the stepfather. Mother and children often have difficulty softening the boundary around the biological family subsystem so that a new member can be incorporated. Frequently, children in single-parent households assume peer-like relationship roles with their parents, which they are loathe to relinquish. They often operate as pseudo adults and, frequently, the residential biological parent is unaware of the degree to which an appropriate family hierarchy has broken down. What must take place is a readjustment of the family hierarchy so that adults are in charge. Children and adults often resist this needed adjustment, perhaps out of habit or fear that the new relationship won't last.

### Adult Years Alone

Adults living alone establish their own rhythm for doing things and make assumptions about how they will live their lives. A dramatic change occurs when time and space is shared with another adult and children. A person who has never been married may never have had to share that time and space, and this may signal problematic issues for the new family.

### Length and Number of Prior Marriages

Some people are just not good marriage material. A number of brief and tumultuous marriages is a signal to the clinician that stepfamily issues, while the presenting problem, may not be the real focus of treatment. (This issue will be discussed more fully in Chapter 9, Vulnerability.)

Someone who has been married before but has no children probably is unencumbered by an ex-spouse, although that earlier marriage may have some financial implications, such as alimony or joint property ownership. No children could mean that contact with an ex-spouse will be limited or nonexistent and will not tug at the new marital relationship. No children also indicates an adult with no parenting experience, an issue that will surely become an area of difficulty when that parent becomes a stepparent.

Longer marriages with children indicate a longer history for those children in another household, with probable inclusion issues for the new marriage. The children and their biological parent form a biological subsystem to which the new stepparent has to struggle to gain access.

## Time Frames Summary

Time frames, composition changes in families and their duration, are indicative of the flow of family process. It is the time frames of separations, the length of the single-parent phase, and the time spent as a single adult or in previous marriages or relationships to which the clinician needs to pay attention. These signal possible problem areas that may surface as relationship hot spots.

## MECHANICS

Mechanics are the nuts and bolts of how things work in the stepfamily. They include issues of custody, support, visitation, and the logistical difficulties created by changes in household composition. Some stepfamilies handle mechanics very well, operating with a degree of flexibility that allows for the occasional changes that seem to be a part of stepfamily life. It is not unusual for us to see stepfamilies where mechanics simply do not become an issue. This usually indicates reasonable relationships between former spouses and across household boundaries.

Where mechanics are an issue, there may be only limited ways to change the reality of the situation. This, however, does not mean that recognition of the issue is unimportant or that attitude adjustments or creative strategies cannot be employed to make people feel better about a situation they can't change.

## Custody Issues

Custody appears to be fixed only because it can be found in a legal document. Most children start out in the physical custody of their mother, but over time, for a variety of reasons, many drift to the father's household. Often there is no legal custody change. If there is something unusual about the custody arrangement, it may signal an important issue. A change in custody, whether formal or informal, should be assumed to be significant. (See Chapter 9, Vulnerability.)

## Support Issues

Child support ought to be a cut-and-dried issue. It should be the financial obligation of both biological parents to care for their children. But, of course, money is an emotionally loaded issue, and what the clinician needs to know is *how* loaded the issue is for this couple. Is child support handled responsibly and conscientiously or is it an issue carrying other emotional baggage? Child support for children who are rarely seen by or who have difficult relationships with their nonresidential biological parent feels emotionally different from support sent to children seen frequently.

If sending child support checks means that the couple is not able to put money away for the down payment on a house, this will be an issue for this couple. It is not unusual for the biological parent to be okay about support and the stepparent to harbor resentment and anger about the money sent to the other household. Child support may constitute a control issue, a signal of an unresolved prior marriage. But don't be too quick to see it only as a control issue; the emotional ramifications can be substantial.

What about a stepparent's financial support of stepchildren? Most stepfathers (because there are more stepfather households) and many stepmothers make significant contributions to the financial support of their stepchildren. And stepparents may also be paying child support for their own children, who live in another household. Many couples have issues about what money comes in and when and what money goes out.

Financial support issues seem the thorniest, although a biological parent's expectation about the logistical support a stepparent will provide may also become a major disagreement because of undiscussed or undisclosed expectations.

## Visitation Issues

We have noticed over the years that some couples show up for consultation in June, shortly before the kids arrive for the summer. These couples want help with the management of visitation, and they usually are very specific about their concerns. For other couples, the issue is weekly or biweekly visitation and how to develop better ways to incorporate these children into the household, to help them feel like "real" family members, and to help everyone deal with the stress of the constant shifts in the household.

For some couples, the issue is a father who pays child support but is effectively prevented from seeing his kids while dealing with his wife's children every day. Another issue is dealing with last-minute changes coming from the other household that mean the couple can never make plans for the weekend the children are supposed to be away.

If children live primarily with their mother and stepfather, does visitation with the nonresidential parent allow for a couple's time alone? Does the couple take advantage of this opportunity? Are there some longer visits during the year that the couple can use to build their relationship?

## Household Composition

There is a logistical component to household composition. It relates to handling visitation issues such as children who have a room of their own except every other weekend when they must share their room with a stepsibling. Stability is elusive during the early stages of becoming a stepfamily, and the achievement of stability is tied to acceptance of the frequent changes in composition and complexity of interactions in the household.

How does the couple address the almost inevitable tension around the shifts in household composition if children visit on a regular basis? How do they address time issues (couple's time, family time, and one-on-one time for parent and child) during the visitation periods? In our clinical experience, logistics and planning are often neglected in stepfamilies, an oversight that is not hard to remedy.

## Mechanics Summary

In the broadest sense, mechanics in stepfamilies are all constant reminders of what some couples call "your previous life," and the obligations that follow parents until their children are grown and beyond. Paradoxically, they may offer the most fruitful interventions, because when changes are possible often they are concrete.

## RELATIONSHIP HOT SPOTS

In a brief intervention, all relationships cannot be explored—nor do they need to be. Relationship issues probably will consume more time and energy than any other topic. We are interested in the hot spots that require intervention and perhaps a changed perspective.

As a society, we make the incorrect assumption that adults instinctively know how to parent. Parenting is shaped by our experiences in our families of origin, but is learned on the job and depends on a parent's willingness to delay gratification because of a child's needs. Our willingness to do this depends in large part on our emotional bonds with the child and perhaps arises from our need to preserve our gene pool. To have no parenting experience and suddenly be thrust into such a position can be frightening and overwhelming, and it creates relationship difficulties for stepparent and stepchild.

Relationship issues do not just revolve around the stepparent and stepchild; the new couple must accommodate their personalities to their developing relationship. They must develop a shared history, a memory book of intimate moments, shared laughter, and obstacles overcome.

### Relationship Issues Related to Primary Residence

Having children in the home full time rather than part time poses very different issues. Opportunities to develop relationships will be more available to stepparents if they have residential stepchildren. However, this situation does seem to push stepparents into parental roles more quickly, with the result that families may move more quickly through stepfamily developmental stages or be stalled more quickly as children resist the addition of a parent.

In our clinical population we have seen a disproportionate number of stepfamilies where the stepparent is pushed into an unfamiliar parenting role and the biological parent is passive or unavailable to help the stepparent with parenting issues. These stepparents do not have the luxury of waiting to establish relationships with their stepchildren before they must assume parenting roles. This situation frequently makes children more resistant and their behavior more problematic.

Pasley (1994) summarized research that indicated that stepfathers of adolescents developed better relationships with them if they were actively involved in parenting, and if limit setting and monitoring (knowing what children are doing, whom they are with, and so on) was done in a warm, engaged style. Our clinical sample has involved many families with acting-out adolescents and we have always taken the position that parents, whether biological or step, must be involved in setting and maintaining appropriate limits with children in the family. Consensus between the couple about limits and consequences is crucial, helping clarify the stepparent role and building the couple team.

However, Heatherington and Clingempeel (1992) suggest that external controls for adolescents may be ineffective if internal controls have not been previously established. Both of us have had the experience of having adolescent clients tell us that while they didn't like limits enforced by a stepparent, they knew the limits were there because the stepparent cared. Because of our personal experience of raising four adolescents simultaneously, we came to believe that an authoritative parenting style was a matter of survival—for us and the teenagers.

Parents in residential stepfamilies often complain that they are the enforcers of homework, chores, and manners, while the nonresidential parents get the fun of weekend activities and a less time-pressured schedule. This can be an area of intervention if the stepfamily is not spending enough family or fun time together.

## Child's Relationship with Biological Parent

The quality of the relationship between children and their biological parents, whether in the same household or not, may be a central determinant of how well relationships develop with a stepparent. If a parent is absent, irresponsible, inconsistent, or abusive, there will almost certainly be profound implications for the stepfamily. If biological parents remain at war, their children will be caught in the crossfire, pressured overtly or covertly to take sides.

Children need access to and contact with their biological parents. If a biological parent is absent or unreliable and irresponsible about visitation, the child may be forced to move into a position of defending the absent parent. It almost seems that the more disappointed the child, the more problematic the relationship between stepparent and stepchild.

Does the couple report that the child idealizes the biological parent? Can the couple help the child identify with a biological parent in realistic ways? What a child believes about why his or her parents divorced is useful to know. Most children believe, at some level, that they are responsible. That belief needs to be changed.

## Relationships Between Stepparents and Stepchildren

As noted above, how this relationship develops will be deeply affected by the child's relationship with a biological parent. We have frequently seen a child's problematic feelings about a biological parent transferred to or projected upon stepparents. The stakes are raised higher when the biological parent is irresponsible, abusive, or abandoning, and this situation will directly impact the stepparent.

A stepparent may want a strong and fulfilling relationship with a stepchild. Often, the stepchild is unable or unwilling to participate in building the relationship. At times, there is a stepchild who wants a parent he or she may never have had and the stepparent may be emotionally unavailable. The question is whether the individuals involved are emotionally available to form attachments.

Sometimes, the stepparent is trying to relate to a child who does not respond. This can be very frustrating and painful and often predicts an eventual emotional withdrawal by the stepparent whose efforts are not rewarded. Can the stepparent say positive things about the stepchild's same-sex biological parent? Is the stepparent supportive of the stepchild having a nurturing relationship with the biological parent? A stepparent's ability to do these things is reassuring and can soften a child's resistance.

If there were any reconciliations after the initial separation of mother and father, children may be waiting for another. If children have been involved in sequential "living together" or remarriage situations they may be unable or unwilling to risk another emotional attachment. We discover that many children in stepfamilies have had multiple relationship losses, including not only a parent but also teachers, best friends, day care workers, and pets.

Even emotionally flexible children will be resistant to permitting themselves to "fall in love" with a stepparent if there have been previous relationship losses. Often, these children set up barriers to relationship development that cause their internalized abandonment issues to replay with the new stepparent. Even when adults truly understand this psychological defense, it can be difficult to endure the emotional testing done by a child who cannot tolerate being abandoned again, yet continually reenacts an abandonment scenario. And if a stepparent is not psychologically minded, this concept may be unacceptable to him or her.

## Relationship Issues for Stepmothers

Women in our society have been socially programmed to act out maternal roles, which often prove problematic in stepfamilies because stepchildren may need to reject nurturing or maternal behavior. Many stepmothers hold very unrealistic expectations about the role they will play in their stepchildren's lives, the activities they will share, and the wounds they will heal.

In our experience, stepmothers who have careers as caregivers, nurses, or teachers seem more vulnerable to hurt from difficult relationships with their stepchildren. Many of these stepmothers are stunned to find a stepchild actively rejecting them. They say to us, "I've never had a child not like me." And because their career is helping and sometimes "fixing" hurt children, they often bring to the marriage fantasies of rescuing and repairing children they view as damaged by the initial marital disruption.

The literature indicates that in stepfamilies the most difficult relationship is between stepmother and stepdaughter (Clingempeel, Brand, & Ievoli,1984), so this is an almost certain relationship hot spot. This can be true even when the stepmother has children of her own. We have found that the stepmother–stepdaughter relationship becomes even more problematic when there is a transfer of a preadolescent or adolescent girl to father's custody (physical or legal). The difficulties seem to be related to adolescence, the reasons for the transfer, and the fact that stepmothers usually are more involved than stepfathers in child care roles in the family. Therefore, they are less able to pull back to a more disengaged stance, a luxury stepfathers may have.

## Relationship Issues for Stepfathers

Heatherington and Clingempeel (1992) report that longitudinal research indicates that stepfathers tend to have a more disengaged style of parenting than stepmothers. This parenting style was helpful with preadolescent children. Once children enter adolescence, more active, authoritative parenting resulted in better relationships between stepfathers and stepchildren. The research found that stepfathers were closer to stepsons acquired when the children were small. It also showed that stepfather–stepdaughter relationships were more difficult than stepfather–stepson relationships. Even in families where the original conflict had receded, that conflict was likely to resurface when the stepdaughter entered adolescence.

## Stepsibling Relationship Issues

There is little information about how siblings respond to divorce and remarriage; there is none we are aware of about the interactions of stepsibling groups. The kinds of issues that our client population reports as relationship hot spots for their children are jealousy of the time or financial resources a biological parent spends with or on a stepchild, jealousy of the parental attention paid to a mutual child, older children feeling that resources are apportioned unfairly in the family, one sibling group ganging up on another, and sexual attraction issues among stepsiblings.

The structure of a child's birth family is changed dramatically in the stepfamily. There may be shifts in ordinal positions from week to week as a child who is oldest or an only child when living at Mom's may be a middle child of a sibling group of four when visiting with Dad on weekends.

## Relationships Between the Households

It is important to convey the idea that cooperation between the two households is something to strive for and will not benefit the children alone. Competition between biological father and stepfather and biological mother and stepmother, whether overt or covert, is important to assess. If it exists, children are often caught in the middle.

Biological parents frequently express their fears that the stepparent will usurp their place in their children's lives; they need reassurance that this will not happen. Biological parents can also be helped to understand that modeling acceptance of the stepparent ("Jane seems like a nice lady.") and giving permission for a child to develop a relationship ("You'll have fun getting to know her.") are enormously helpful.

## Difficult People

Sometimes relationship hot spots are not simply a function of stepfamily dynamics but also result from people who have difficult personalities dealing closely with one another. Temperamental difficulties in children or inflexible adults will certainly compound stepfamily issues, but the management of these relationships may hinge on temperament or personality rather than on addressing specific stepfamily issues.

What is a stepparent's personality style? Is it cooperative or competitive, rigid or flexible, emotionally distant or nurturing? An individual's personality provides the canvas on which relationships are painted. The concept of goodness of fit between stepparent and stepchild is useful as it does not make a perfect fit the only acceptable relationship outcome.

## Relationship Hot Spots Summary

In corporations there are divisions that operate efficiently and profitably as well as divisions that need attention, whose performance does not add to the bottom line. In stepfamilies, some relationships function better than others. It is the relationships that create tension and ongoing problems that become a focus of intervention. Attention to these relationships will ultimately improve family functioning, the bottom line for families.

## SUMMARY

As we noted in the beginning of this chapter, it is the structural elements of composition, time frames, mechanics, and relationship hot spots that provide much of the clinical background needed to form hypotheses about what the significant issues are (or will be) for the stepfamily that has consulted you. These structural components need to be viewed as a normal part of the stepfamily context and process.

# CHAPTER 5

# *Expectations*

## ASSUMPTION #4: EXPECTATIONS AND BELIEFS ABOUT HOW THE STEPFAMILY AND ITS MEMBERS WILL OPERATE NEED TO BE EXAMINED AND SHIFTED TO A MORE REALISTIC PERSPECTIVE.

If we conceptualize a paradigm as beliefs and expectations about how something works, then a person's acceptance of the realities of being a stepfamily member is truly a paradigm shift. This shift includes changing beliefs and expectations about what is possible for the family, accepting the reality of the situation, and understanding that this new family cannot be expected to heal old hurts.

It is often the unrealistic expectations of stepfamily members that hamper appropriate development of a new family identity by the family members. More realistic expectations are required before families can move through the necessary developmental sequences to the stage where stepfamily issues no longer need constant attention. (See Chapter 3, Developmental Processes.)

Accepting more realistic expectations also entails a fundamental shift in beliefs about what it means to be in a family, and how family members relate, so that stepfamilies can be viewed as "normal" families. This shift has to do with what it means to be in a stepfamily and what can be reasonably expected from the other members of the new family.

## UNREALISTIC EXPECTATIONS

Underlying our unrealistic expectations about stepfamilies are our tenaciously held beliefs about family. Emily and John Visher have shared with us, in several personal conversations, their belief that the intense emotions generated in stepfamilies arise because all of us have expectations about how our most basic human needs will be fulfilled in our families.

Our need to be nurtured, to have a sense of acceptance and inclusion, to be fulfilled in our relationships, to see our efforts recognized, and to hope for the sharing of common goals are universal expectations about being part of a family. Of course these needs often are not met fully in our families of origin, but most of us believe that they ought to be. If they have not been met, we are even more vulnerable in a stepfamily situation to wishing and wanting to be included, accepted, and fulfilled.

If we think about these universal needs in the context of stepfamilies, some of the difficulties experienced by stepfamilies begin to make more sense. The insider/outsider dynamics of the stepfamily often prevent inclusion and acceptance, especially during the early stages, resulting in emotional distance, anger, and feeling stuck as family relationships don't develop as anticipated. And it is during the early stages that people's expectations are highest, not yet having shifted to more realistic, achievable levels.

Given this perspective, the intense affect clinicians encounter when they work with stepfamilies becomes normalized, and they can respond more empathically to stepparents who expected to get these needs fulfilled in the stepfamily but who are not yet allowed by the biological subsystem to be part of the group/family. Without this perspective, it is easy to see these intense emotional reactions as "crazy."

Informing families about people's basic human needs and how they are played out in the stepfamily also broadens the stepfamily context and helps stepfamily members feel less crazy about the intensity of their reactions. Indeed, in our experience, it is usual for people to react with relief to information that normalizes their emotional responses.

> You mean, I'm not crazy? I really thought there was something wrong with me; these feelings would wash over me and it was like they didn't belong to me. I'm a nice person, how could I have such awful thoughts?
>
> —Stepmother of one year

We believe that the intensity of emotional reaction often seen in stepfamilies leads to incorrect and pathological diagnoses being made of people who are having normal reactions to an extremely difficult adjustment. If clinicians do not know about stepfamily dynamics, it is easy to put two and two together and get ten.

Mala remembers a stepmother telling her with great shame that a year and a half into her remarriage she had become so angry with her elementary-school-age stepchildren's defiance about cleaning their rooms as requested that she pulled their mattresses off their beds, pushed all the stuff from their rooms down the stairs into a pile, and then pulled the mattresses on the front lawn. Her husband was stunned and furious when he came home. The children were frightened at her rage, and she felt tremendous guilt and shame about her out-of-control behavior.

Clearly, this was not a productive way to express her feelings; however, when viewed in the context of her stepfamily, her *emotional* reaction did not seem so extreme. She had no children of her own and married a man whose wife had died leaving three small children. A housekeeper/nanny had been in place for three years, hired to care for the children during the wife's terminal illness and after her death. When the new wife moved into the house where her husband and stepchildren had lived, she was relegated to a position below the housekeeper.

At her husband's request, she had quit her job to stay home and take care of the children, but she was not allowed to do so. Every effort to be nurturing and maternal was rebuffed by children, husband, and housekeeper. Every attempt to put something of herself into the home was greeted by upset from the children and anger from her husband, who thought she should be more understanding of the children's needs to have everything remain the same. Attempts to prepare meals or change things in the kitchen were reported by the housekeeper to her husband, who then criticized her.

Systematically, she was shut out of becoming part of the family and had found no way to get her husband to listen to her feelings. Putting all the children's things in the living room and their mattresses on the front lawn got her husband's attention, finally.

Internally, this woman felt crazy and her behavior made her appear crazy to her husband. It took some time to help her husband understand the depth of her pain at being excluded from the family. Providing the context of normalcy and informing husband and wife that the intensity of her feelings was understandable because her need for inclusion was being denied helped them to come to an understanding of her feelings and behavior.

The husband was able to see that part of his unwillingness for her to be part of the family was unresolved grief about the loss of his first wife. He was also able to acknowledge the energy and effort his wife put into getting his attention, and they jointly agreed on signals the wife would use, signals he agreed would not be ignored.

*Unrealistic expectations create:*

- intense feelings and reactions
- disappointment
- anger
- emotional distance
- feelings of being unappreciated
- barriers to relationship development
- barriers to intimacy between couple
- a "too little, too late" attitude

**Exhibit 5.1. Effects of Unrealistic Expectations.**

Although this may seem an extreme example, it is unusual perhaps only in the public display of the stepmother's upset. A front yard full of mattresses is hard to ignore. However, the degree of distress she felt is not unusual as we have seen in the 15 years we have worked with stepfamilies. In fact, keeping in mind our assumption of normalcy, we would say that this stepmother's *emotional* reaction to her situation was predictable.

To sum up the effects of unrealistic expectations in stepfamilies, see Exhibit 5.1.

## REALISTIC EXPECTATIONS

One of the tasks for therapists in the Step By Step model is to create a context for the individuals in a stepfamily to shift their beliefs and expectations about such families. For this shift to occur, we believe that educational input about the difficulties of the process must be made available to clients, and their efforts must be validated. Whether this information is presented by a clinician or generated in a support group setting, it will permit family members to understand and better tolerate the discomfort of the intense feelings and emotional reactions so common to the early stages of stepfamily life.

When we accept that education normalizes the process, making it more tolerable, we create the context for the necessary shift in expectations. Education also provides some emotional distance from the topic and can provide a forum for dialog and sharing of feelings that may otherwise be quite difficult.

Exhibit 5.2 lists some of the positive results of shifting beliefs about stepfamilies. Often expectations need to be lowered drastically. This creates the climate for a win–win situation, where the only way to go is up. If a stepfather has minimal expectations about what sort of relationship he will develop with a stepchild, a child's acknowledgment of his entry into a room will be experienced as a move in the right direction rather than "too little, too late."

## ERRONEOUS BELIEFS ABOUT STEPFAMILIES

Most unrealistic expectations are grounded in beliefs (myths) people hold about stepfamilies and how they operate. Modifying expectations comes about by a thoughtful examination of beliefs and expectations, reality-based education, and suggestions for ways to modify the beliefs.

### First-Marriage Families Are the Best

> I can't believe I introduced myself to everyone at the wedding reception as the wife of the groom's uncle. In my head your first wife is still David's aunt, not me.
>
> —Mala Burt, stepmother of 10 years

All of us have some sort of family internalized in our psyches. And most of us, if we are honest with ourselves, think that there is only one kind of "real" family (the intact, first-marriage family) that is truly acceptable.

---

*Realistic expectations create:*

- emotional openness
- a climate for appreciation and validation
- potential for change
- receptiveness to any degree of effort
- appreciation of any positive change

---

**Exhibit 5.2. Effects of Realistic Expectations.**

We must pay attention to this belief because it is pervasive, persistent, and simply untrue.

This belief is the underpinning of denial and shame about divorce and remarriage, and it is fostered by many subtle social reinforcements such as being "second best," the pejorative use of words naming step relationships (stepchild, stepmother, stepfather), and our cultural heritage of fairy stories such as Cinderella and Hansel and Gretel.

Many stepfamilies respond to this social pressure by pretending they are first-marriage families and using the same last name for all the children. The public education system has also sent similar messages, and it is only recently that schools have begun responding appropriately to the no longer occasional occurrence of four parents wanting to attend back-to-school night and meet their child's teachers.

The fact that half of marriages today end in divorce does not diminish the feeling of failure that often accompanies divorce. This perceived failure leads to guilt, and sometimes to massive denial. Mala tells the story of the time she told Roger that her brother had confided in her that he and his wife were contemplating divorce. "You know," she commented, somewhat conspiratorially, "If he gets a divorce, it will be the first one in my family." Roger looked at her in amazement, exclaiming, "You're divorced!" "Oh, right. I guess I forgot," was Mala's response. First marriages can't be erased so easily, but the shame and sense of failure of divorce is sometimes difficult to acknowledge. We believe that the sense of failure is often grounded in an internalized belief that first marriages are best.

## I Love You So I'll Love Your Kids

> I'm a kindergarten teacher. All my students adore me, and I love all of them. What's wrong with me that I can't warm up to John's little girl? She's cute and smart and well behaved for a four-year-old. Why can't I feel more connected to her?
>
> —Stepmother of 18 months

Stepparents frequently start with the expectation that they are not only going to like their stepchildren, they are going to love them. Sometimes there is a wonderful chemistry between a stepparent and stepchild, but more often the chemistry is of the explosive kind at the beginning.

When you marry someone who has children, you expect to care about your stepchildren. And we are not talking about just taking care of them, being fair and equitable as if you were a teacher in charge of some students you don't really like. The expectation of most stepparents is that they quickly will become emotionally connected to their stepchildren. When this doesn't happen, stepparents feel guilty. Their emotional reactions are frequently incongruent with their personal beliefs about what kind of a person they are. This can create a scenario where stepparents become angry and resentful, even mean, when children are not as emotionally responsive to their overtures as they expected.

We tell stepparents that the first thing you have to do is get along. Then, you have to allow time for relationships to develop. You may get to like each other, maybe you'll get real lucky and even love each other someday, but lowering your expectation about instant love allows you to take the time needed to let a child come to you. Mutual respect between stepparent and stepchild is an acceptable and laudable outcome. Stepparents have to overcome (or outwait) whatever adjustments and resistance children bring to the new family. You cannot overcome their resistance by a full court press.

## Divorced Kids Never Get Over It

> I saw in the paper recently that kids who've gone through a divorce have a lot more emotional problems. Poor Danny. Every time he gets into trouble, I know it's because of the divorce. It's the reason he's been in so much trouble as a teenager and doesn't do well in school. He just never seemed to recover after his Dad and I split up eight years ago.
>
> —Biological mother of a 16-year-old

Children whose parents divorce and remarry commonly experience developmental delays, but most get back on track in time. In our opinion, they are not permanently emotionally damaged as many people seem to believe. In reviewing longitudinal surveys from Great Britain and the United States, Cherlin et al. (1991) concluded that "much of the effect of divorce on children can be predicted by conditions that existed well before the separation occurred" (p. 1388). Anderson and White's study (1986), which looked at characteristics of intact families and stepfamilies, suggested that functional families have common characteristics, as do dysfunctional first-marriage families and dysfunctional stepfamilies. While Heatherington and Clingempeel (1992) found adjustment difficulties for children in stepfamilies, they concluded that "while marital transitions may place children at risk for adjustment problems, the emergence of problems is not inevitable and is likely to be related to other factors than just family status" (p. 72).

Certainly, there are children who temperamentally are less flexible and have more difficulty adjusting to change. These kids will have more difficulty. And we are not saying that kids don't react to divorce. What we are saying is that we do not believe that children are irreparably damaged because of parental divorce. Parents who engage in postmarital warfare of one sort or another damage their children because the divorce is never over. Most parents work hard to be reasonable and responsive to their children through this difficult time, but no parent is able to be there 100 percent all the time.

Because parents feel guilty about getting out of an unsatisfying marriage, they often excuse and explain unacceptable behavior as a reaction to the divorce. Danny's mother excuses her son's troublesome behavior as a by-product of the divorce and does not see her inability to set appropriate limits or adequately supervise his behavior as part of the problem. Poor school performance is blamed on unresolved divorce issues, and so no one checks to see if there is a learning problem, not enough parental supervision of homework, or too many hours of television. Guilt about her divorce from Danny's father means that she has a hard time holding Danny to task, which prevents him from understanding that he is responsible for his behavior. When viewed in this light, problems become a parenting issue rather than a child's ongoing reaction to a divorce and remarriage.

Many of the families who come to see us have poor parenting skills and don't believe that they have a right to set limits with their children's behavior. They sometimes have a hard time believing that limits are a safety net for children and actually help kids feel safe because they know that a parent is in charge. Parents sometimes have difficulty distinguishing the difference between allowing a child to express feelings and permitting those feelings to be acted out.

## Wicked Stepmothers, Abusive Stepfathers

> Our first Christmas as a new stepfamily, our children were given copies of Hansel and Gretel by three different sets of relatives.
>
> —A stepcouple of six years

When we conduct stepfamily workshops for clinicians, we write the words stepmother, stepfather, and stepchild on a blackboard or flipchart and ask participants to give us the adjectives that come to mind. "Wicked, uncaring, mean, evil, abusive, molesting, neglected, left out" are words that are always called out, reflecting commonly held beliefs about stepmothers, stepfathers, and stepchildren. If there are clinicians in the audience who are also stepparents, they often acknowledge that while they know that they try hard to be nurturing, caring, and fair, the words that come to mind are still the negative ones listed above.

There is evidence that children are more at risk of being murdered by a stepfather or the new man in their mother's life than by a biological father. Daly and Wilson (1992) discuss violence in stepfamilies and present a Darwinian view that the lack of genetic and emotional bonds probably puts stepchildren at more risk than biological children to be abused verbally, physically, or sexually. These situations are tragic for all involved but *the reality is that the vast majority of stepparents are people trying their best to help raise somebody else's children.* And there is not much societal support for this difficult role, perhaps because the media focus on the small number of sensational cases rather than on the ordinary stepfamilies where people are doing their best.

## Adjustment to Stepfamily Life Happens Quickly

Life has been such a roller-coaster ride for the last two years. Melanie tries hard to get along with the kids, sometimes too hard, in fact. She says I ignore the way they treat her. I guess I'm just used to them being obnoxious at times. I thought we might have it rough for a couple of months but it seems to get harder, not easier.

—Biological father, remarried for three years

Because they are in love and marrying so they can be together, most people have the expectation that their love will facilitate a rapid family adjustment—a "we're happy so everybody will be happy" fantasy. The reality about the time it takes stepfamilies to develop comfortable ways of being together is very difficult for families to accept. It is not the way they want it to be. It is when they get discouraged and disheartened, we believe that they are more likely to end a marriage prematurely. People tell us, "I've been through this once. It was awful, but I survived and can survive again. I didn't get married to feel this torn up."

This belief about quick adjustment means that people who are unaware of stepfamily dynamics interpret the long period of adjustment as something they are not doing right, a problem in the marital relationship, a mistake in whom they picked to marry, and so on. They will seize on anything to try to understand why the family doesn't meet their expectations.

Clinicians must educate their clients about the developmental stages stepfamilies go through but they must exercise some caution when conveying this information. If we tell couples in the first session that it takes most stepfamilies four to seven years to develop comfortable relationships and reliable family rhythms, they may become discouraged and afraid. After all, if they are three years into the process, feeling overwhelmed and discouraged, they don't want to think life may not feel better for another four years or so. Clinicians need to remember that clients usually come for treatment when they are feeling the worst and should convey this insight to those clients as well.

Education about the developmental sequence is the key because it normalizes the process and gives hope for a better future. This education can take the form of information given during a session or material to be read between sessions. Couples must be able to put themselves in the process and maintain a sense of hope about getting to more comfortable territory. They need to understand that this is an evolutionary process and the discomfort will not last for the entire three to seven years.

This is another area where a clinician acts as guide and coach. "I know you are going through a rough time right now; let me help you understand why it feels so difficult. This stage is not permanent and here is what you can look forward to in the future. It takes time to develop a family history, which is what you are doing all the time you are together, and with that will come a sense of family identity. It is not possible to do that in three months or a year. It takes as much time as it takes."

## Withdrawal of Biological Parents Helps Children Adjust

If their Dad would just move to Alaska and leave us alone, we'd all be better off. Joey and Erika can't seem to get connected to Don, who acts more like a father to them than their real Dad ever did. This every other weekend thing is hard on them too. They always seem to be recovering from a visit or worrying about the next one. Sure they'd miss him, but they'd get used to it.

—Biological mother in a stepfamily for two years

The belief that children adjust to divorce and remarriage more easily if the biological mother or father withdraws often is based on a residential parent's discomfort or anger at having continued contact and sharing a child with a former mate. Parents also agonize over the child's discomfort with the situation. Sometimes it is wishfulness on the part of non-residential biological parents, who frequently feel tremendous pain over not being with their children full time.

We have had a number of biological parents ask about the wisdom of withdrawing from their child's life because it seems so difficult for the child. When the obvious is pointed out, "This must also be extremely difficult for you," nonresidential parents usually are able to talk about their own pain. An explanation of the psychological ramifications of such an emotional abandonment, of a child's developing sense of identity based in some part on a positive regard of both biological parents, and of strategies for dealing with emotionally difficult visits usually clears up this difficult issue. It really is important for parents to stay connected, no matter how difficult the circumstances.

Roger was consulted by a mother who was concerned about her 7-year-old son. She had recently remarried and her son had a tenuous but developing relationship with her new husband. Her concern was her child's continued contact with his father, who was doing jail time for selling drugs. A number of issues were discussed, including the emotional and physical safety of the child if he were to visit his father in prison and the need to explain on an appropriate cognitive level why his father was in jail.

The mother didn't want continued contact with her former husband; she explored whether it was possible that another responsible adult could oversee the child's visits with his father. Ways of staying in touch when people couldn't be physically together were suggested, such as letters, videos and/or audiotapes, and photographs. Situations such as this must be addressed on a case-by-case basis using common sense as well as applying a theoretical perspective about children's reactions to perceived parental abandonment.

It is not uncommon for stepcouples to say that all of their problems would be over if an (expletive deleted) ex-spouse would move far away or drop dead. Learning to deal with an ex-spouse around child issues is extremely important. It also is extremely helpful if the biological parents can pull together and form what Emily and John Visher call "a parenting coalition." This means the biological parent and stepparent in each household can work together on behalf of the children when necessary and appropriate. While this is not always possible, it is an important goal for stepfamilies. Clinicians can assist couples by presenting co-parenting and cooperation between households as a reachable goal.

We prime couples to think that even if this goal is not achievable now, it may be possible at some point in the future.

## Stepfamilies Formed After a Parent Dies Are Easier

> Cassie was just three when her mom died, and she can't remember anything about her. She's been without a mom for seven years and is getting to the age where she really needs one. You know, to explain about girl things. In a way this will be much easier because we won't have the weekend interruptions and the constant comparisons.
>
> —A stepmother-to-be

As a clinician you are aware of the problems inherent in this belief. However, many lay people will not understand that this scenario generally creates more difficulties because there are no reality checks for the children. They can fantasize about how wonderful Mom or Dad was, often elevating the parent to sainthood. This lack of a reality check means that they never experience that parent as irritable, upset, or too busy to pay attention. The parenting attempts by a new stepparent are discounted. "My real mom would never have made me do chores on Saturday morning before I went out to play with my friends."

The effort to develop connections with a stepparent may be sabotaged by a child who feels disloyal to a deceased parent. The stepparent's own unrealistic expectations about the situation may propel him or her into a more active parenting stance than is advisable.

For the couple there are multiple problems. We have heard many reports of new wives or husbands moving into the households where their new partner had lived with the former spouse. They "inherit" the house, the children, and the furniture; they may find that they have moved into a shrine. Taking down pictures, especially those of the deceased spouse, or rearranging furniture may precipitate a crisis with spouse and children who are not ready to have a spouse or parent seemingly erased from the household. It is more difficult for people who have suffered the permanent loss of a loved one to move forward and integrate a new person when they may still be grieving or when changes reactivate the grieving process. It can feel disloyal for adults as well as for children.

It is not just houses. It is all the other baggage people bring to new marriages, baggage that is not necessarily emotional. Clinicians must listen carefully for symbolic issues. A reluctance to get new living room furniture may be connected with feelings that memories of a deceased spouse or parent will go away with the old couch and easy chairs. It can be hard to accomplish nesting when most of the twigs had been chosen by someone else who came before you. With time the symbolism may wane, but in the early years there may be constant symbolic reminders of not being the first.

A client recently told Mala that she had moved into a house that her husband and his first wife had built. Carved into the living room mantel were their initials and the anniversary date of that first wedding. Because his first wife had died, the new wife felt that for the children's sake she couldn't push the issue of getting a new mantel. But it remained a sore spot. If this couple had consulted Mala years earlier, they would have been advised to make a joint decision about the mantel. If the decision was to remove and replace it, the children should be reassured that it was being stored so that one of them could have it some day. However, this woman's intuitive response about not removing the mantel right away was on target. To do so too quickly probably would have been very upsetting for the children.

## Part-Time Stepfamilies Are Easier

> If we don't get some time to ourselves soon, I'll go crazy. We've been married for a year and since Mary Jo's kids' father lives on the west coast we've only had a week alone since then. I sure envy families where they only have to deal with kid issues every other weekend.
>
> —Residential stepfather of one year

By part-time stepfamilies we mean those where the children visit rather than reside most of the time. Families with residential stepchildren may envy families where children only come on weekends. They forget that relationships take time to develop and it takes time to develop a family history. If a child is in your house two weekends a month, you've got 24 occasions during the year to build family history. If the children are adolescents, they probably will exit the family before new family relationships and identity can be formed.

The stark reality is that both residential and nonresidential stepfamilies have challenges inherent in the structure of the family—who resides where and when. Relationships in residential stepfamilies may be built more quickly or may more quickly reach a boiling point and boil over. A stepparent and stepchild in a nonresidential stepfamily may want more time together, or they may find the limited time a blessing. It depends a lot on the personalities of the adults and children.

Parents who don't live with their children don't drop off their emotional connections when they drop off the children. Nonresidential parents worry and fret, too; they want to be able to help with homework and make sure their kids don't eat too much junk food. Not being with your children is sometimes a relief, but it is experienced by most nonresidential parents as a loss of emotional connection and control.

Clinicians must be careful about what they hold out as goals for these families and must recognize that any number of outcomes may feel satisfying. Ask clients what *they* hope to have happen. Do these hopes and the concurrent expectations need to be moderated?

## Being in a Stepfamily Is Easier If You Are a Mental Health Professional

> You'll love being in a stepfamily. It'll be just like the Brady Bunch.
> —Mala Schuster and Roger Burt to their four children,
> prior to their wedding in 1975

> I don't care where your mother put the cereal bowls, Justine, I want them on this shelf.
> —Mala Burt, stepmother of six months

> Do all little boys tussle like puppies on the living room floor? The girls never act like that.
> —Roger Burt, stepfather of six months

> Your ex-wife *still* has one of your credit cards....?
> —Mala Burt, remarried for one year

These are just a few of the statements we'll admit to. Our only excuse is that 20 years ago nobody knew much about how stepfamilies operated. For clinicians who are part of stepfamilies, there are the often awkward moments when they find themselves doing something and knowing better. Just knowing about stepfamily dynamics doesn't mean that you won't fall into some of the same traps as everyone else, that you won't feel the same intense feelings and frustrations. Everybody who is in a stepfamily has to work hard to make the family work.

## SUMMARY

We've talked about the process of becoming a stepfamily and the notion that one of the clinician's jobs is to help the stepfamily become aware of and more comfortable with the process of becoming a family. What we are really talking about is tolerating the discomfort of the shift in beliefs and expectations until an acceptance of the reality of stepfamily dynamics can be achieved, creating movement towards the necessary paradigm shift. When individuals change their beliefs and expectations about stepfamilies (and about families in general), they become more aware of the possibilities of getting their most basic emotional needs met in this new family context.

Recognition and acceptance of the difficulties inherent in getting these needs fulfilled paves the way for creative strategies that may create more opportunities for fulfilling these goals. This internal shift also allows individuals to acknowledge that some of their needs may not be met at particular times or to recognize that perhaps these needs will never be met in the way they hoped in this particular family context. A change in internalized models of family and how families work is crucial for satisfaction with the evolving reality of the stepfamily.

Family members must move toward acceptance of the new family norms that are being developed. A new family identity is the ultimate goal for the family, but this is not a realistic goal for a brief intervention such as the Step By Step model. Rather, working towards acceptance of the similarities and differences among individuals in the family group is the goal. Movement in this positive direction implies a decrease in or cessation of comparisons with an unrealistic and idealized family form. Acceptance of the occasional discomfort posed by the process is crucial.

# CHAPTER 6

# *Goals of the Step By Step Model*

## ACCEPTANCE OF THE STEPFAMILY PROCESS

The overall goal of the Step By Step model is to help families understand and accept the stepfamily process, develop ways to tolerate the discomfort of the adjustment process, maintain a future orientation of hope, and accept the idea of a good enough fit for relationships in their new family.

This overarching goal is achieved by focusing on small, manageable changes in beliefs and behavior and acquiring knowledge of the stepfamily process that validates and normalizes the reactions and efforts of family members as they move toward a "new family culture" (Visher & Visher, 1988, p. 21). Clinicians must understand that this model intervenes at particular points in the stepfamily process, and that achieving a new, unified family culture or identity (a new sense of family) is not a realistic goal in this brief treatment model.

Even when the adjustment process is complete and stepfamily issues are no longer the focus of the family, each member of the family will have a different sense of the family depending on a number of variables such as age, position in the family, and role as it has evolved. Whatever sense of family is achieved is acceptable as long as family members are comfortable with the resolution and family functioning. As with many stepfamily variables, there is no right or wrong way to be a stepfamily. Satisfaction is measured by the comfort levels of the individuals and how well the family meets members' perceived needs. We do not assume that there necessarily will be agreement among all family members about how successful the family adjustment has been.

The Step By Step model assumes that this new sense of family or the final stages of stepfamily adjustment will not be reached while the mem-

70

bers of the family are relating to the clinician. The stepfamily adjustment process is long and diverse. The goals of the Step By Step Brief Treatment Model are well defined and more concrete, involving specific goals related to the functioning of the couple, the children, and the family.

## A COUPLE'S MODEL

The Step By Step model is based on interventions with couples. Treatment always begins with the couple, regardless of the presenting problem, because of our belief that the family survives and flourishes only if the couple does. Only when a partner refuses to come do we begin with an individual. In our experience, the most effective interventions occur when one is working with the couple—usually the most fragile bond in the family. Strengthening this relationship and facilitating functioning of the couple team decreases the likelihood of another marital disruption, and this outcome serves the whole family.

Visher and Visher (1988) and Papernow (1994) write of the effectiveness of seeing the couple, but also note that at other times they see dyads, family groups, or the whole family. Sager et al. (1983) suggest a supra-system model (particularly when a child is presented as the problem) that is not feasible in many private practice or agency settings. Many of our clients come to us after having been seen by someone who started with the whole family, with the result that the fragile couple bond was weakened rather than strengthened. Subsequent chapters will deal with situations when we would include other family members or perhaps see the whole family.

You will notice that although we begin by seeing just the couple, we think in terms of a family perspective. Our dialog with couples offers an unspoken suggestion that changes made by the couple will ripple out and positively affect the family as a whole. For example, when starting a session, we might ask, "How is the family doing this week?" rather than, "How are the two of you doing this week?" This may be somewhat confusing in our text as most of our interventions are with the couple, but we think and tend to speak about a context that includes the whole family.

## GOALS FOR THE COUPLE

The principal goal for the couple is strengthening their relationship so there can be a successful navigation of the lengthy stepfamily adjustment period and a prevention of divorce. A number of ways to strengthen the couple relationship are discussed in the next two sections.

## Build a Couple Team

The achievement of effective functioning as a marital and parental team is crucial to the success of the family. A clinician accomplishes the goal by building on the strengths of the individuals and on the couple's interactive strengths. Do they have common goals? If not, can they find common ground? How do they divide tasks? Do they celebrate their successes or do they slip away unnoticed? Are they able to focus on what needs to be changed? Do they prioritize well? Collaborate? Review progress? If lacking in any of these areas, couples can benefit from discussions of how to build an effective marital partnership—helpful to the survival of first marriages and crucial to the survival of stepfamily unions. The following areas need to be assessed.

### Create a Solid and Effective Boundary Around the Couple

Visher and Visher (1988) and Papernow (1994) write about the need for appropriate boundaries or delineations around the various subsystems in stepfamilies. In the stepfamily, the boundary around the couple must function differently from the boundaries around the children. The children's boundaries must be permeable, because they must allow access to nonresidential but biologically related family members. The new couple needs a firmer boundary that helps separate and protect them as they develop their relationship—which has less history than parent–child relationships and is often experienced as more fragile.

### Develop Communication Skills

What kind of communication skills does this couple have? Is improvement needed? Does this couple listen to one another? Do they mind read? Do they check with one another if an issue is unclear? Can they agree to disagree? Do they know how to negotiate a compromise? If not, they need to be given these important tools.

### Use Limited Energy Wisely

Individuals in stepfamilies have limited energy because of their complicated families and the adjustments that must be accomplished. Couples must learn how to expend their limited energy and time on issues that will give the greatest payoff. This concept and technique will be discussed in Chapter 8, Triage Assessment and Management.

## Develop a Couple's History

Couples in stepfamilies have the added burden of developing a marital and relationship history at the same time that they are adjusting to the new stepfamily. It is important to help couples understand the necessity of setting aside time for themselves. Time is a valuable commodity, and while many couples talk about the lack of time very few actively plan how to schedule it.

We talk to couples about making time to hang out the way they did before they were married. Hanging out time is defined as time that is planned but unstructured. It could start out as a walk around the block but might evolve into a drive for frozen yogurt. Couples also need time to plan and dream. The purpose of spending time is to develop a relationship history, and couples must make a conscious effort to take the time they need to establish and build the marital relationship. Taking time often must be preceded by making time, which means scheduling unplanned relationship time. Couples often have difficulty with this concept and tend to believe spontaneous happenings are better. Our message to them is that time for themselves as a couple will rarely, if ever, happen if they don't plan for it.

## Create Glue in the Couple Relationship

The glue that strengthens the couple relationship and assists them in functioning more effectively is the aggregate of loving gestures, thoughtful glances, considerate responses—the experiences of a relationship that stick people together. It is what helps hold couples together through the difficult stepfamily transition. We suspect that all clinicians have some similar concept by which they predict whether a couple will be able to repair a marriage, weather a serious problem or navigate a treacherous transition. As clinicians, we gain a sense of this somewhat vague concept by watching body language, how couples communicate, the degree of respect and humor in the relationship, the quality of the commitment to the marriage.

We believe that couples who have little or no glue in their relationship have little chance of surviving the stepfamily adjustment. Even couples with a lot of glue may need help setting marital relationship priorities. Again, the emphasis is on effective functioning as a couple team as they relate to and manage a difficult family situation.

## Improve Family Management

Implementing family management strategies includes establishing an appropriate family hierarchy, if one is not already in place. Most of the stepfamilies (indeed, most of the families) we see have hierarchy problems. Sometimes these are so severe that repairs must be made here before stepfamily issues can be addressed. More frequently, the issue seems to be that parents need reassurance that it is appropriate for them to be in charge of the family. Parents in stepfamilies need guidance on how to accomplish this in view of stepfamily dynamics. Setting limits and consequences is only one part of the parents being in charge.

Accepting responsibility for the emotional and physical safety of their children is also a part of this responsibility, and sometimes it means telling kids they can't do what they want to do. As one father told Roger, "I thought about what we talked about last week, you know, how the kids seem to be in charge in our house. I think you're right that it needs to be us. Our neighborhood, you know, it's a war zone—not a safe place for our kids. I figure Maggie and I gotta be the generals or the kids might not make it."

These were parents whose guilt about their divorces and remarriage had led them to allow their kids to make decisions that jeopardized their physical safety. Children learn to take advantage of parents who don't want to disappoint or deprive kids whom they view as having been through a lot.

## GOALS FOR THE FAMILY

The primary goal for families is to strengthen family relationships. Achieving a new sense of family involves acceptance of what the family means to each family member. That sense, as noted previously, will vary considerably from person to person depending upon each person's place in the family, stage of development, and needs. Relationship and family history has to be developed. Dyadic relationships within the family and family activities have to be encouraged. We must help our clients remember that building history takes time.

The initial therapeutic goal for the family is to achieve a new stability. It is the couple who must bring this about through their improved functioning together. Often, we see this new stability coming about within a matter of days following the initial consultation. It is this key element that typically leads to a short course in therapy.

## Build Functional Teams

The couple must be a functional, as well as the primary, management team, and it can benefit from skill development in this area. In reality, a variety of functional teams usually develop or can be nurtured. Positive interactions create an opportunity for the clinician to highlight what is developing well. Parent–child relationships continue to develop and evolve in ways that are appropriate for the developmental stages and they need appropriate maintenance. There also can be functional relationships that develop between a stepparent and stepchild because of a common interest or need. Surprisingly, the children from different families often work well together as another team, giving support and comfort as well as offering friendship. There may be conflicts in these stepsibling teams, but actions for mutual benefit are also common.

Clinical literature often lays heavy emphasis on dysfunctional alliances within families. There are issues of enmeshment and dysfunction, such as overly close parent–child relationships based in the single-parent family phase. Such relationships can be viewed as structural and almost inevitable to some degree, but they should not be initially viewed as pathological. They can change with proper management. Not all attention needs to be on the difficulties.

## Build Relationship Histories

There are no shortcuts to building relationship histories. They are built minute by minute by sharing time together. Each interchange, either verbal or nonverbal, adds to the history. Sharing activities that may or may not have goals is one way to take the time necessary to build a relationship. So often the focus in new stepfamilies is on family activities, but we cannot emphasize enough the importance of one-on-one time to accomplish the necessary task of building personal relationships within the new family.

As with couple's activities, one-on-one time must often be planned. With children, it doesn't need to be much time, perhaps 10 to 30 minutes. But we suggest that the time commitment be honored by the adult. If the child doesn't want to participate, do not force the issue; just indicate that you hope he or she will want to participate at the next scheduled time. This approach takes into account the need many children have to proceed slowly with new relationships.

## Build Family History

Like building relationship history, building family history involves building memories of shared experiences. New stepparents need to be sensitive to children's (and sometimes a partner's) need to talk about similar
experiences in the prior family. Many families consciously choose activities that are not emotionally loaded with memories. Be prepared for a
variety of reactions from children, depending on their ages. Adolescents
may not want to participate in a day-long or weekend activity. But we
think it is fine to insist, for example, on some shared family time or some
meals being shared.

Creating new family traditions and rituals can be a satisfying part of
building a family history. When looking at traditions and rituals, look at
what can be added rather than abandoning experiences that are comforting and provide stability in the family. And be on the lookout for
activities that can become ritualized as part of the culture of the new
family. These rituals, even when insignificant on the surface, become
attached to our expectations about how our family operates and give us
that necessary sense that we know who we are and who is part of our
family. For a complete discussion of ritual in families see *Rituals in Families and Family Therapy* (Imber-Black, Roberts, & Whiting, 1988).

We have been a stepfamily for 20 years, and for most of those years we
have celebrated Thanksgiving at Mala's mother's home. As the children
have grown and left home the group has waxed and waned, depending
on people's ability to get back east. The menu changed somewhat as
Mala's mother aged and began asking people to bring different parts of
the meal. Last Thanksgiving, one of Roger's daughters came from the
west coast; after the dinner, she asked Mala privately, "Where were
Grandma Milly's homemade rolls? I'd been looking forward to them for
weeks. Why did we have store-bought rolls?" Clearly, to this daughter,
Thanksgiving dinner was not Thanksgiving dinner without Grandma's
rolls. This is a small but significant part of our family history. To Kira we
are, among other things, a family who has homemade rolls for Thanksgiving.

We also tell our clients the story of how divine providence inter-
vened at our first Christmas together. We had gone out and chosen a
tree; now it was in the middle of the living room floor and ornaments
from the Burt household box and the Schuster household box were
being carefully hung. Everything was lovely—until we got to the top of
that first tree. Out of the Burt box came a star and out of the Schuster

box came an angel. Promptly, the children began squabbling. "All real Christmas trees have stars at the top," Justine insisted. "Well, *our* Christmas trees were real trees and we always have an angel at the top," shouted Thomas, the oldest. Then we noticed that the tree we had picked had two terminal branches, one for the star and one for the angel. And ever since we have looked for Christmas trees that would accommodate both.

## GOALS FOR THE CHILDREN

The principal goal for children is to assist them in resuming normal, age-appropriate development. Rather than viewing the children as pathological as they wrestle with the multiple adjustments associated with divorce and remarriage, we prefer to view them as needing to divert their energies during these events. As they deal with crises, their normal childhood development may be deferred. As things begin to come under control, they resume normal development and catch up to where they should be.

Frequently, children are presented as the problem. In many cases, the clinician can assist the couple in helping their children through the adjustment process by readjusting the family hierarchy, teaching parents better listening skills, and offering concrete suggestions for other kinds of support for the children. Often, we prefer that the parents act as therapists and, with some guidance, many can do this very well.

### Create a Climate Where Children Can Express Feelings Appropriately

Children need to be able to have such feelings as grief, loss, frustration, unfairness, or being in the middle, without being told to stuff or deny their feelings. When a couple comes for a consultation, the family often is still in the early stages of transition. Children typically have emotional work to complete, especially mourning the losses they have suffered and dealing with the feelings about new changes in their lives. It is not in their best interest to shut down their feelings. But at the same time their feelings need channelling and structure, permission and control. Parents can help by removing the scare associated with these feelings and assisting children in working through the feelings in a safe environment.

## Help Children Effectively Utilize Guidance

This involves recognizing what the children are feeling, helping them reflect on their feelings, and coaching them about appropriate ways to act on their feelings. With more education about stepfamilies, parents can often point the way to the issues for the children. And when the couple feels more under control, they can listen to the children's feelings more effectively.

If children are to navigate the stepfamily transitions successfully, they will need guidance about expressing their feelings. "We can talk about this, but yelling and calling names isn't allowed." "Sometimes I feel like crying, too. Sometimes I do, and sometimes I listen to my favorite music when I'm missing the old neighborhood."

Kids also need education that will assist them the same way it does adults, normalizing the process. Parents may underestimate what it takes for a child to make a successful transition, to begin the process of managing and healing old wounds.

What we have noticed is that as reasonable parental authority is restored within the family hierarchy the parents are in a better position to foster expression of feelings and give guidance. They can relate better to the children's behavior, the development of relationships, and expectations about behavior. The children can then receive effective guidance regarding family issues. Guidance is much easier when the crisis has diminished. Parents often need help knowing how to dampen a crisis, or how to keep everybody safe while putting out fires.

The breakdown of the first family, the single-parent phase, and all the issues between these events and remarriage may have confused or disturbed the family hierarchy. The couple needs to establish themselves at the peak of the hierarchy again with appropriate authority and an effective partnership as together they nurture and guide the children. Despite their protests, often the reinstitution of the hierarchy is a great relief to the children, who are then freed to resume their own lives as children. Inappropriate responsibility is lifted from their shoulders. We believe that this change has a lot to do with the marked improvement at home that parents often report after only a few sessions.

## Establish Permeable Boundaries Around Children

As previously stated, it is in children's best interest to have access to their other parent. We believe the children of divorce who make the best adjustments are the children who have the most reliable contact with their nonresidential parent. This means contact the child can count on whether that is a visit every three months or every other weekend, or knowing that Dad will call at 7 P.M. on Wednesday nights. It seems to be the reliability that is so reassuring to children whose lives have been disrupted.

Children need to be reassured about continued and reliable contact with their other parent and movement through permeable family boundaries as they enter and leave their different homes. Creating appropriate boundaries around the children also permits a firming of the boundary around the adult couple.

## SUMMARY

Accepting the stepfamily process means tolerating, at times, more than occasional discomfort. Of course, no family is uncomfortable, or for that matter, comfortable, all the time. It is our belief that recognition of the unique characteristics of stepfamilies will help people tolerate the differences, as does understanding that some stages of the transition may be more uncomfortable than others. The act of naming the discomfort (and the reason for the discomfort if this is known) creates emotional distance that makes people more comfortable. Recognition of the reality that most people in stepfamilies experience similar discomfort also makes the uncomfortable times more bearable.

Helping a couple achieve and maintain a future orientation permits them to create plans and dreams that fuel their enthusiasm for the long, hard work ahead. A future orientation is essential for stepfamily couples because so many activities are deferred to children's needs at a time when the couple is striving to solidify their relationship. Even in a first-marriage family, there will be little left for the couple after the children leave if they share no future dreams or plans.

Future orientation is even more crucial for a stepcouple because the quality of the couple's relationship is what makes this effort worthwhile. Over and over, we hear individuals tell us, "I wouldn't put up with this grief, all the problems we've had with the kids over the years, except that I'm crazy about Tony. If it weren't for him, I'd be long gone." Using a future orientation supports the "light at the end of the tunnel" image we hear constantly. There must be a reason for the marriage to continue beyond getting through today's challenges.

Parent–child relationships are described as healthy if there is a good enough fit between the personalities and temperaments of parent and child. This is a useful concept for stepfamilies. Relationships don't have to be perfect and people don't always have to get along. Tolerance of differences and relationships that work most of the time are attributes of a good enough fit in a stepfamily. Often, unrealistic expectations put higher demands on stepfamily relationships than would be placed on first-marriage relationships.

The couple is primary and leads the way. The achievement of a strong and stable marriage benefits the couple, as does giving their children the advantage of a stable family. The children, who do not get the fantasy of the reuniting of their biological parents, get the supreme benefit of being able to resume their normal childhood, and sometimes young adulthood, development. Ultimately, each member of the family achieves a new sense of family that is appropriate for him or her. Table 6.1 is a representation of these concepts.

## Table 6.1
### Clinician's Guide to Stepfamily Intervention

---
*Assumptions*

---

- Stepfamilies Are Normal Families, Valuable and Viable in Their Own Right.
- Developmental Processes Drive Stepfamily Adjustment.
- The Structure of the Stepfamily Predicts Issues That Will Be a Focus of Treatment.
- Expectations and Beliefs About How the Stepfamily and Its Members Will Operate Need to Be Examined and Shifted to a More Realistic Perspective.

---
*Tasks*

---

- Accept and Understand Normalcy of Stepfamily Experiences and Reactions.
- Understand Developmental Issues for Family and Individuals.
- Understand Issues Growing Out of Structure of Stepfamily: Composition, Time Frames, Mechanics, and Relationship Hot Spots.
- Examine and Modify Expectations and Beliefs as Necessary.

---
*Goals of the Intervention*

---

- Goal: Strengthen Couple Relationship
    Build a couple team
    Develop couple history
    Improve family management
    Create couple "glue"
- Goal: Strengthen Family Relationships
    Build functional teams
    Develop relationship histories
    Develop family history
- Goal: Resumption of Children's Normal Development
    Express feelings appropriately
    Utilize guidance
    Establish permeable boundaries

---
*Goal for the Stepfamily*

---

- Goal: Understand and Accept Stepfamily Process
    Tolerate occasional discomfort of process
    Maintain future orientation
    Accept idea of "good enough fit" for stepfamily relationships

# CHAPTER 7

# *The Initial Intervention:*
# *The Stepfamily Assessment Guide*

The Stepfamily Assessment Guide provides a framework for the initial intervention in the Step By Step model. The clinician must quickly gather information about the stepfamily being presented and make informed decisions about the focus of the intervention while educating the couple about the stepfamily process. See Exhibit 7.1 for a list of goals for the initial assessment.

The initial intervention in the Step By Step model is what we term an assessment intervention. It is an interactive assessment, providing the clinician with opportunities to introduce normalizing and educational statements about the stepfamily process. The assessment differs from more traditional psychosocial intake assessments in that we do not expect to gather all important life history information. In traditional training, an intake interview might take one and one half hours or more, with the goal of gathering information for the purpose of formulating a diagnosis.

Because we do not use a medical model, the primary goal is not diagnosis, although for insurance purposes we must attach diagnoses to clients to secure third-party reimbursements. In most of our stepfamily cases, one partner can be accurately diagnosed with a reactive depression, anxiety, or adjustment problem. Just keep in mind that diagnosis is not the primary goal of the initial assessment interview in the Step By Step model.

Clinicians need to be able to identify stepfamilies who will benefit from the Step By Step brief therapy model, as well as stepfamilies or individuals who may need more extensive treatment because of their

- Join with the clients
- Create an opportunity for controlled ventilation
- Create a genogram
- Assess the family context
- Normalize stepfamily context
- Establish goals for this intervention
- Provide educational materials

**Exhibit 7.1. Goals of the Initial Assessment.**

family structure or personal history and families or family members who need to be referred for other kinds of treatment. (See Chapter 9, Vulnerability.)

## FOCUS OF THE ASSESSMENT

The information that must be gathered in this rapid assessment can be divided into five categories: composition, time frames, mechanics, relationship hot spots, and other. The focus of the information is the history of the new family, how long it has been together, and how it functions. The kinds of responses given will quickly help the clinician focus on areas for intervention (for example, relationship hot spots) that will assist the family in better understanding and tolerating the stepfamily process—the primary goal of the model.

We find that for many couples the normalization of the stepfamily process, which can be accomplished easily in the assessment, decreases stress and tension dramatically. Clients find that the issues they are struggling with are *common* and *expected*. They begin to acquire a time frame for the process, and so they immediately begin to adjust their expectations. Frequently, they leave that appointment unexpectedly hopeful about the future.

Do not lose sight of the core assumption of normalcy. If this couple is basically normal, the functioning of their relationship and of their family will begin to improve dramatically with a brief intervention. If it does not, one person will gain the spotlight and demonstrate the need for special attention. Sometimes a couple's functioning improves dramatically, but there still may be a child who stands out as having distinct problems. In most cases, we see rapid and often dramatic improvement.

We urge you to deliberately gather a bare bones family history. An elaborate and lengthy history either will be unnecessary (because of a swift, positive reaction to treatment) or can be obtained later if focus must be shifted. In either event, the pursuit of the assumption of normalcy permits economy of effort.

The assumption that there is a developmental process for stepfamilies presupposes stages. It will be important for the clinician to have a sense of where in the developmental sequence a given family and individual may be. In our experience, stepfamilies most frequently present toward the end of the early stage of the stepfamily developmental sequence. The clinician must be alert for families who are stuck in a stage or who have not adequately completed a stage, and they must note whether all members of the family are in the same stage. For example, if a couple have been together for eight years and are still in the early stage of stepfamily development, their development has ceased or been warped by some other factor. If a couple married and then devoted years to a custody dispute, their energies will have been diverted. Only when their focus can be shifted will they begin individual, marital, and family development again. In effect, they may be at the beginning of their marriage when they come for help. It is important to note that this family would not be viewed by us as pathologically stuck, but rather as an example of a delayed adjustment because of external forces. We also want to note that with intervention, this couple might have been able to attend to relationship and family development issues at the same time they dealt with the custody dispute.

The structure of the stepfamily, the key players, where they live and the nature of the relationships among them constitute vital information to gather. Probably more than any other information, it is these structural components that alert clinicians to probable relationship hot spots for the individuals, couple, and family. It is in an individual's reactions to stepfamily issues that we begin to see repetition of historical patterns. If more historical information is necessary, the need will quickly become apparent.

Expectations drive perceptions and reactions. They can create optimism or dictate hopelessness. The educational process begins at the very beginning of the first session because we have an opportunity to make educational and corrective input while gathering information. Thus, intervention and adjustment of expectations begin at once. We also always give couples a copy of *Stepfamilies Stepping Ahead* (Burt, 1989), a publication of Stepfamily Association of America, Inc. This small, readable book is full of useful information about the stepfamily process. We ask couples to read it between the first and second session. If they do, they gain valuable insights into stepfamily dynamics. If neither has read it by the next session, we have some information about the lack of commitment of this couple to their relationship and family. For couples seen for just a few sessions, this book serves as future reference material.

Do not forget that we assume psychopathology is not the force driving these individuals or their family unit. If these are normal people experiencing a normal developmental crisis, and if there are no hidden impediments or agendas, expectations can be adjusted quickly and a comfort zone will be created to allow family members to better tolerate the process of becoming a stepfamily.

## THE STEPFAMILY ASSESSMENT GUIDE EXPLAINED

The Stepfamily Assessment Guide is offered as a framework for the initial assessment intervention. Underlying the guide are the four core assumptions discussed in Chapters 2 through 5. The goal of this assessment intervention is not to know everything about each person in the family and certainly not to know every problem each one has. The focus is on finding out the most important information about this new family. In this guide, the questions quickly focus on the most important issues for stepfamily clients, which can be divided into four categories: composition, time frames, mechanics, and relationship hot spots.

Some questions will be more important to the clinician than to the clients. An example would be, "How old were the children when parents first separated?" To the adults, the date of the divorce may be the more important date, but when a clinician is assessing a child's possibly stalled development, the separation question is more to the point. In other areas, the adult couple will guide you because they are usually quite clear about the most problematic areas. For example, a couple will usually be able to tell you about relationship hot spots that need to be a focus of attention.

Because the focus moves so quickly to educate, adjust expectations, and inform, the first session may be exceedingly chaotic. All the information on the Stepfamily Assessment Guide may not be gathered and it may not be reasonable or possible to gather it in the order listed. Gathering information in an inflexible order may cause you to abandon important issues that may require immediate intervention or at least comment. It is a good idea to recheck the rapid assessment guide between the first and second sessions to see if there are obvious missing pieces, interesting holes, or intuitions that should be pursued in the second session.

We have included an unannotated version of the Stepfamily Assessment Guide to allow you to read through it quickly and gain a sense of the information being gathered. Following the guide is an annotation, complete with comments, explanations, and suggestions for use.

We offer several caveats about the initial assessment. Information will almost surely not be gathered in order. The complex and chaotic nature of most stepfamily histories has a tendency to sidetrack the interviewer. Use these diversions to educate the family, normalize the stepfamily process, and focus the intervention. Don't despair if you don't get all the questions answered. Clients are generally quite clear about their major concerns.

### STEPFAMILY ASSESSMENT GUIDE

Clients Present: The stepcouple.

Interview strategies: Ask the stepfamily magic question, encourage controlled ventilation, obtain genogram, perform clinical interview, and develop the clinician's perceptions.

#### COMPOSITION

   I. Obtain genogram.
     A. Obtain basic current family structure.
     B. Note areas that may indicate problems.
     C. Basic people-related information.
       1. stepcouple
       2. children
       3. ex-partners
       4. stepsiblings

#### TIME FRAMES

   I. Length of marriage or relationship (current and previous).
  II. How long ago did separations occur?
 III. How long between separation and divorce?
  IV. How long between separation and remarriage?
   V. How long as a single parent?

#### MECHANICS

   I. Custody arrangements:
     A. How was decision arrived at?
     B. What does the separation agreement say about custody?

    C. Have there been modifications to custody (in fact or legal changes)?

II.  Visitation:
    A. What are the legal parameters of visitation (what is in the separation agreement)?
    B. What is the actual visitation as it occurs?
    C. Have there been changes in the visitation schedule?
    D. Were the changes agreed to by both biological parents?

III. Child support:
    A. Are the legal agreements being honored?
    B. If not, what are the problems with child support?

## RELATIONSHIP HOT SPOTS

I.  Relationships:
    A. Sequence of marriages or long-term relationships
    B. Never married
    C. Other children from prior relationships
    D. Other significant relatives

II.  Soundness of relationships of children with biological parents:
    A. Relationship
    B. Irresponsibility
    C. Physical or emotional abuse

III. Nature of relationships in the family:
    A. This couple
    B. Adults to adults in other households
    C. Adults to children
    D. Children to children

## OTHER

I.  Couple Details—in many interventions this type of information may never surface. Examples include:
    A. How did they meet?
    B. Work history
    C. Family-of-origin capsule history

II.  Financial situation:
    A. Have they bought a house together?
    B. Money handling (one pot or two pots)

III. Special Issues:
    A. Child with physical, long-term emotional or learning problems.
    B. Anyone in this or extended family with significant health problems or substance abuse problems?

C. Anyone in the family treated for or in need of treatment for emotional problems?

D. Anything else clinician needs to know about?

E. Have you gone elsewhere for help? What happened?

These questions reflect the basic informational goals of the initial session or sessions. You can see that the type of information being gathered is specific and focused, generating a clear picture of the developmental process and structure of the stepfamily and information about beliefs and expectations.

## ANNOTATED STEPFAMILY ASSESSMENT GUIDE

The initial assessment pulls together pieces of a complicated puzzle, allowing the clinician and the clients to begin to formulate opinions about which pieces are most important and where intervention is needed.

## Clients Present: The Stepcouple

Usually, the person calling for an appointment is the female head of household, most often the stepmother. Frequently, the presenting problem is a child. Even in these situations, we prefer to see the couple for the first intervention, to gather information and to get an idea of how the couple relate. Children are not included so parents can speak freely and give a complete history, including information about former spouses it might not be appropriate for children to hear. If a caller's partner is unwilling to come to an appointment, we encourage the caller to make an individual appointment and to invite the partner.

## TECHNIQUES FOR ASSESSMENT

## Encourage Controlled Ventilation

Controlled ventilation is the concept of venting feelings and frustrations, but in a way that does not attack or denigrate other family members. Clinicians should step in if they see ventilation operating inappropriately and make corrective suggestions about more appropriate ways to share feelings. The clinician also needs to control the amount of ventilation; usually we limit it to no more than five minutes.

Ventilation often begins the moment the session starts. Emily Visher suggests asking, "Tell me about your situation," which we see as the stepfamily version of "The Magic Question" of brief therapy fame. This seemingly benign question often unleashes a floodgate of emotion and information, especially information about what couples see as their most critical problems.

Many times couples have told no one about the distress they are feeling and often there is a great deal of shame and self-blame attached to what they perceive as the problems in the family. Immediately, there is the opportunity for educational input. Often, what couples see as a problem can be reframed as normal in the stepfamily process.

## Clinical Interview and Clinician's Perceptions

The clinical interview provides a format for asking many questions, as well as the opportunity to observe a couple during the interview process, giving you important information about a couple's level of distress, their empathic responses, and a demonstration of their styles of relating and their ability to communicate. This gives you information about relationship strengths and about areas needing improvement. All of this is important to know when you begin to formulate interventions.

A clinician's perceptions of a couple are part of the information being gathered. Do you feel overwhelmed? Do you feel hopeful or hopeless about their situation? Does the couple seem committed to working on the problems? Do they show the capacity to learn during the assessment interview?

## INFORMATION TO BE GATHERED

## Composition

Obtaining a genogram provides information about who is in the family system. It is a visual tool for storing information about a family. For those of us who are visual learners, it is an invaluable method of obtaining and recording much of the structural information we need. It is fast and easy, and we encourage you to develop your own methods and symbols.

A genogram doesn't have to be neat and tidy and the symbols don't have to correspond to any particular system (e.g., McGoldrick & Gerson, 1985).

The genogram provides you with a handy reference guide to the current family structure and serves to highlight possible problems. Use this visual diagram with its record of people's names and ages, step, half, and biological relationships, former marital partners, and time frames as a "cheat sheet" in sessions. Most pertinent information will be recorded here. Roger's genogram is quite basic and reflects the format he finds most useful, which includes time frames information such as length of marriages and when separations occurred. Other information is included in his intake note. Mala's genograms have notes written in the margins, perhaps including a phrase that captures a theme in the family. We are including examples of Roger's and Mala's methods of recording information. (See Exhibits 7.2 and 7.3.) As you can see, these are idiosyncratic. We encourage you to develop your own style. Whatever works for you is all right.

An unexpected bonus the stepfamily derives from making a genogram is that it provides a concrete visual representation of how complex their stepfamily system actually is. For some families, this is the first time they can see that the confusion and chaos they feel is appropriate to the complexity of their family system. (Note: when a child later becomes the client, we have found it useful to make another genogram with the child. Even young children can be very good reporters, knowing much more about the family than one might imagine. Usually one of us does the drawing, laying a big sheet of newsprint on the floor or coffee table in the interview room. You will want to keep a copy of this genogram, so make two if you think the child will want to take one home.)

## Time Frames

*Time frames* give us vital information about beginnings and endings. You can speculate about possible issues based on information about time frames.

### From Beginning to End

The length of time spent in a marriage or the time that has passed since an initial marital separation has different meanings for individuals in a household. If parents separated when a child was 11 months old and the

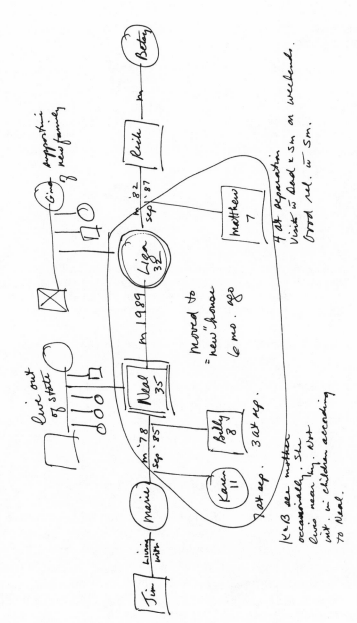

Concerns: ① Karen & Billy re: mother ② Neal & Liza — gone/time
③ marie - boundary issues

Jim — living with → Marie
m '78
sep '85

Neal
35

Billy
8

Karen
11

3 at sep.

3 at sep.

live out
of state

Ginger apprentice
& new frame

Liza
32

m 1989

moved to
= new frame
6 mo. ago

matthew
7

m '82
sep '87

Rick

m → Betsy

7 at separation
Visits w Dad & Sm on weekends.
Good rel. w Sm.

Kr B. are mother
occasionally. She
lives nearby. Not
int. in children according
to Neal.

June 1990

Exhibit 7.2.   Example of Mala's Genogram Style.

| | | |
|---|---|---|
| Phyllis—6 years<br>Not remarried<br>Has legal custody of<br>  both children<br>Visitation irregular<br>Separated 9 years | | Paul—6 months<br>Not remarried<br>Visitation every other<br>  weekend<br>Separated 5 years ago |
| Ron—39 | M—1½ months | Karen—32 |
| Janie 11<br>Physical custody 1<br>year<br><br>Brad 14<br>Physical custody 3<br>years | | Cara 5<br>Legal custody<br>Resides with Karen |

*Note:* Couple is in the center with marriage noted in middle. If they have any children together, they would be listed in the bottom center section. The placement of the children in the boxes shows where they are living most of the time. The years after the ex-spouses refers to the length of the marriage preceding. Comments about visitation and other issues will be written in that section. Length of time of or when separation occurred is listed in the upper boxes. Other pertinent information related to a given person may be written in the appropriate section.

**Exhibit 7.3. Example of Roger's Genogram Style.**

child is now four, the child has no memories of parents being together and a shorter relationship history with the residential parent. A 14-year-old whose parents separated two years ago has more relationship history with biological parents and is also dealing with the complications of adolescence.

### Time Between Separation, Divorce, and Remarriage

In terms of assessment, the time frame from separation to remarriage is the important one. How long ago did the separation occur? Legal divorce usually is not the issue unless someone is separated for years prior to obtaining a legal divorce. It is the physical separation that triggers the most intense emotional reactions. For adults, it makes the decision real. For children, separation is the signal that the family unit is dissolving and life will change significantly. You need to get an idea of what life was like before the separation and from the separation to the remarriage.

Besides the absence of a parent, how did life change? What were the effects on the family and individuals?

These questions probe the issue of how this time has been filled. Has it been acrimonious and full of legal wrangling and frequent court appearances? Can you speculate about why these people did not get over their divorce and get on with their lives? We all know couples who have a legal divorce but remain as emotionally attached as if they were still married. An incomplete divorce creates boundary and attachment problems in remarriages. Fred's new wife will probably have some feelings if he still mows his ex-wife's lawn and balances her checkbook.

Were there reconciliations? How long did they last? Reconciliations create desperately desired hope in children who want their parents back together. Even if a couple later divorces and remarries, children's hopes about an eventual reconciliation may just be rescripted. "I know they'll get back together eventually. You know, they did when I was little. It'll just take time," Joey, age 9, tells Roger about his parents who have both remarried. This difficult-to-relinquish hope is one of the reasons we do not advocate trial separations for couples with children—either first marriages or subsequent remarriages.

Remarriage is a signal event to children, because it affects their fantasy that biological parents will reunite. When both parents remarry in a short period of time, the adjustments a child must make are multiplied. The remarriage of a single parent raises issues for the parent as well. He or she must learn to share the parental hierarchy with someone else. Not only is the parent unused to sharing parenting, but the children will almost certainly resist. The predictable rhythm of the household will be upset until a new rhythm can be established, a process that can take a long time.

### What Was the Duration of the Single-Parent Household?

Long years in a single-parent household permit the children to expect an exclusive relationship with a parent. When this parent remarries, children will fight not to have their relationship disrupted. A boy may be strongly ensconced as the little man of the household; a girl in Dad's custody after her mother's death may have become quasi wife and mother to younger children. Daughters can be fierce competitors for Daddy's affection, as any stepmother with a 12-year-old stepdaughter can attest. Pay particular attention to an assessment of whether the children are successfully navigating the adjustment process. Are behavior, school performance, and peer relationships back to normal—or at least moving in that direction? Two to three years is a reasonable amount of time for younger children to get back on track. Pre-adolescent boys seem to take longer than girls to recover from divorce, although problems may emerge again for girls as they go through adolescence. Girls may have more difficulty adjusting to the remarriage of the parent with whom they live. Heatherington & Clingempeel (1992) indicate that adolescents may have more difficulty adjusting to a parent's remarriage, but also hypothesize that their 26-month-long study may not have covered a long enough period to track adolescent adjustment.

We have seen many children whose emotional development, in some areas, seems to have halted at the time of the original parental separation. Clinicians need to attend to this, as it can explain children's behavior years after a separation. In our brief therapy model this is information to be passed on to the adult couple, along with suggestions about how they can help a stuck child get back on track. Depending on your assessment, children may need to be referred for more evaluation and/or possible individual or family treatment.

## Mechanics

Mechanics are the nuts and bolts of how the family works. They include, among other areas, the logistical arrangements a family makes and how they were arrived at.

### Custody Arrangements

The clinician will want to know how custody decisions were made. Was it the result of a 6-year-long legal battle or a 20-minute discussion? Actually, both of these scenarios are problematic. Protracted legal maneuvers put life on hold for all concerned, but a too-quick decision about custody may signal an uninvolved parent. Is there any evidence that children are being used as spoils of war or tools of revenge? There will be conflicts even for well-meaning and concerned parents who are divorced, but their ability to put personal issues on a back burner when a child's needs are at stake is a good indication that remarried households will be able to communicate appropriately when necessary.

What does the separation agreement say about custody? It is often interesting to compare what is in the legal documents and what is in fact happening. Once again, the legal issues are important only if you are going to court. Clinicians want to know what really is happening. A lot of agreements are made outside of the courtroom. When parents can be cooperative, decisions affecting the children can be made without the time and expense of involving the legal system.

Have there been modifications to custody, real or legal? In many states, joint custody is the arrangement of choice. However, in most instances the children have primary residency with one parent, usually the mother. Has the primary residency of the children been changed? Was this a precipitous occurrence or was it planned? In our practice, many families seem to undergo informal shifts of residency. Sometimes a child is gradually or precipitously turned over to the nonresidential parent, often the father. We know that this is a component in our profile of the most vulnerable stepfamilies, stepfamilies in which the father has physical custody of the children.

It is not uncommon for sons, sometime during their adolescence, to spend time with noncustodial fathers. In many instances, these are cases where mothers are no longer able to manage or control an adolescent male, and experience a sense of relief at the change of residency.

In contrast, the turning over of children at the beginning of a remarriage can signal a revenge motive. A newly married couple recounted their dismay, the morning of their wedding, at receiving a call from the husband's former wife saying, "I put the kids on a plane this morning. They'll arrive in Baltimore at 2:35 P.M. Oh, and by the way, enjoy your honeymoon." A sudden shift in residency of a teenage girl may signal serious problems in the mother–daughter relationship, or a teenage girl who has lived with father and stepmother may precipitate a move to her mother as a way of getting reconnected with the nonresidential parent.

We are not opposed to planned changes in residency for children, even when there is not a concomitant change of legal custody. If parents can cooperate and the child's needs are considered, such changes are not harmful.

## Visitation

What is in the separation agreement about visitation? What are the legal parameters? Highly restricted visitation mandated in court documents can reveal issues of abuse, power, or revenge. Ask about the separation agreement because it may signal a problem area where a couple's energy is being unproductively expended. Flexible visitation, developed independently of the separation agreement, may reflect a mature relationship between ex-spouses that has developed over time. This is not unusual and it can signal cooperation between households that benefits all involved and means that the new couple will not have to expend energy in this arena.

If we are asked for a recommendation about visitation, we counsel that if a divorced couple is still having trouble communicating with civility, it is best to leave the agreement as it is spelled out. Both parties need to be aware that this leaves no room for flexibility, even when it would benefit them. We also make people aware that many couples work their way toward a flexible schedule that takes into account the sometimes last-minute scheduling changes that occur for older children and responds to emergencies or special occasions in both households.

A 15-year-old may prefer to be with his friends rather than with Dad and stepmom on weekends. A midweek visit with an upset child may be indicated, as might a trip to McDonald's to celebrate a good report card. An out-of-state parent may be coming through town on a business trip and be able to spend a few hours with a child in an airport lounge. We see flexible visitation as a goal because it provides children with the most access to both parents and is possible only when there is cooperation and communication between households—both desirable goals. However, it is more likely that you as a clinician will be called upon to help a couple cope with problematic visitation.

What is the actual visitation as it occurs? One of the advantages for a couple in a complex stepfamily is that coordinated visitation may be possible, leaving the couple childless on some weekends. Irregular, unplanned, or missed visitation is, in our view, emotionally injurious to children, who may restrict their lives while waiting for a call or visit that rarely comes. Additionally, if visitation is infrequent or last-minute, the couple may rarely have any time for themselves and logistical problems result as plans cannot be made or must be changed or canceled at the last moment. For a couple trying to find time to nourish their new relationship, this can be very trying. And they will almost surely also be dealing with an upset child.

As mentioned previously, it is important to attend to issues around visitations that are difficult or cannot be enforced. The courts do not link child support and visitation and we have seen instances where men (and occasionally women) pay child support regularly, but the courts fail to support and enforce visitation. In these instances, the biological parent, usually a father, finds himself dealing with stepchildren on a regular basis, but is unable to see his own children. There may be an emotional playout in the stepfamily that deserves attention.

Have there been changes in the visitation schedule? Changes can signal an improvement in the climate of parental relationships, a deterioration, or simply the fact that because of circumstances a change was needed. Again, we take a nonpathological view of changes in visitation unless changes are the result of putting an adult's needs before a child's or of coercion by the other parent. You want to know why changes have occurred, whether the changes were agreed to by both biological parents, and if the changes were in the child's best interest.

## Child Support

What are the problems with child support, if any? The information you are seeking here is whether child support issues are creating problems for the couple in your office. Is child support being used to attempt to control a former spouse? Is this a situation where a nonresidential mother is responsible for child support? Failure by a biological parent to honor legal agreements about support can be an economic and emotional stressor in the new family.

In our opinion, children rarely understand these issues. When they are small, they do not have the cognitive abilities to understand, they just know they hate the upset. When children are older, there may need to be candid discussions of the reality of the child support issue. Clinicians should counsel parents about the need to be evenhanded in setting out the realities of irregular or nonexistent support. If there have been problems or if problems are anticipated we often recommend that support go through the court system, which provides some emotional distance about this issue and puts enforcing compliance into someone else's hands.

Not infrequently, support is an issue for couples when a new husband believes that "your ex will never pay on time because he knows he can get away with it and you'll never do anything about it." This kind of thinking turns support into the responsibility of the mother rather than of the children's father. Support can also be a loaded issue in the stepfamily household where the children visit. It is this household that sends the check every month, or is supposed to. Feelings of resentment about the amount of income that goes to support another household (the way it often feels) may be a divisive issue. We have been told by a number of couples in which the husband has several children from a previous marriage and the new wife is childless that the reason they do not have a child is because they cannot afford to because of the amount of child support they pay. What a dilemma!

Stepfathers often feel that they are a major source of support for their wives' children, even when child support is regularly paid. They may be essentially correct, but children's needs must be viewed as part of the package deal of remarriage. A stepparent's feelings about this issue may need to be ventilated safely. Irate parents who must fight for child support are often unable to abstain from ventilating to their children about how irresponsible the nonsupporting parent is. This is difficult and hurtful to children. The child often responds by becoming emotionally protective of the irresponsible parent. This is an emotionally charged issue that speaks more to an unfinished divorce than anything else.

*Note on Custody:* As clinicians we have no interest in becoming embroiled in custody disputes. We make our position on this clear in the first interview, sometimes in the first telephone contact if we hear signals that we are being consulted in order that we may be used as expert witnesses. We tell clients that we don't go to court and that if we are subpoenaed we will be hostile witnesses. We offer to refer to someone who may have an interest in testifying if we think that this is what the client has in mind. It is easy to get embroiled in these disputes, but the minute you take sides you have lost your ability to be objective. Joining with clients is one thing; siding with clients is something else.

## Relationship Hot Spots

In stepfamilies, there are some relationships that seem to be more problematic than others. Information about composition will often predict relationship hot spots.

### Multiple Relationships

What is the sequence of marriages or long term relationships for each partner? Is this a second or a fifth marriage? How did previous relationships end? Divorce or death? How long ago? If previous marriages ended in divorce, ask why. Of course you are getting only one side of the story, but it will give you a piece of the puzzle. Was communication the problem or infidelity? Or did people simply outgrow each other? Was the separation amicable or hostile? Did individuals have adequate time to grieve and regroup between relationships? Did this new relationship begin before the previous one ended? Any of these questions may provide hot spot information.

The sequence of relationships also affects children and predicts possible relationship hot spots. If the children have experienced a series of relationships and divorces, they may have little belief that a new marriage will endure and may be able to generate little enthusiasm for a union that feels so right to the adults. Given the divorce rate among remarried couples, the children may be wise in withholding their feelings, at least for a time. We believe that many children cannot begin adjusting to a remarriage until their belief that this family will endure has been strengthened by time and experience. The number of relationship disruptions experienced by children may be predictive of the amount of time it takes them to incorporate a stepparent into their lives.

### Nonparent Partner

This presents an issue for both men and women, but in our vulnerable stepfamily profile it seems to affect women more often than men. If there is no child, there is no parenting experience and no child to validate one's parenting efforts. The stepmother without children often feels that she has a thankless job and frequently receives her validation only through the thanks of her husband. There will almost certainly be unrealistic expectations about getting to know stepchildren and about the ease of the stepparent's assimilation into the household. Adults may make unrealistic assumptions about their parenting skills or how quickly they will assume a parenting role. For men, the symbolic issues often concern passing on values they perceive the children lack or the validity of their authority in the home. For women, symbolic issues may concern not being the first to share certain experiences with a partner—particularly childbearing and child-rearing experiences. This issue can become very concrete if a childless partner decides that he or she wants children and the other partner, who already has children, does not want to consider this option.

### Children from Prior Relationships

These include the children who are present or who visit, but may also include children who haunt the family and are never present. A stepfather or stepmother may be asked to perform a parental role, enduring the pain of knowing that he or she already has children who have emotionally slipped away. A parent may have chosen not to stay involved or may have been shut out by a vengeful former spouse. Sometimes, this pain surfaces only after a couple has married or moved in together. The pain may intensify and become unbearable. A child given up for adoption or a terminated pregnancy may haunt a stepmother who is now unable to conceive. Miscarriages and stillbirths can also profoundly affect remarriages. Usually, this information is not gained in an initial assessment. It is more apt to surface later if a couple can't seem to progress through basic stepfamily and couples' issues. We have even seen several cases where children were not acknowledged until after a remarriage. Needless to say, this degree of information management does not make these couples likely candidates for our brief-therapy model.

### Other Significant Relatives

Do any other relatives live in the couple's household? Sometimes these individuals won't be mentioned unless you ask this question specifically. It is easy to ask when doing the genogram, "Does anyone else live in your household?" As you complete the genogram you can also ask "Is there anyone else important to the family whom I should know about?"

Grandparents can be a blessing to stepfamilies when they offer time, tolerance, and fair treatment of all children. However, a doting grandparent who favors biological grandchildren can be very divisive, creating problems when birthdays go unacknowledged or holiday gifts are very discrepant. A couple once told us of a grandmother who was willing to pay for a family portrait every year but demanded that the picture exclude the second wife's child from her first marriage. The real problem for this couple was that the husband wanted to accommodate the request. Handling divisive and disruptive relatives is an area where a stepfamily couple often need helpful suggestions about setting appropriate limits and, possibly, strategies to include a relative in a way that would prove less problematic.

Sometimes an ill relative or a chronically ill child who lives in the home or is the responsibility of one of the adults can take up so much time and energy that little is left for developing new family relationships and history. In this case, it is not the relative who is the problem, but rather the demands made on the limited time a couple and new family have to spend together.

### Soundness of Relationships of Children with Biological Parents

The basic essence of the relationship between the biological parent and child needs to be probed. How the child relates to each parent is crucial to an understanding of the pressures being played out in the family being assessed.

Irresponsible parents pose very real problems for the other parent.

If Mom or Dad shows up irregularly for visitation, what is the other parent to say? Reassuring a child that "Daddy loves you very much" can be confusing but denigrating the irresponsible parent hurts the child. The child's hurt needs to be addressed.

We think that most residential parents can help their children even with these difficult scenarios. You can educate the concerned parent about children's responses to such a situation and script responses suitable to the child's age and situation. Parents need to understand that idle reassurances leave a child vulnerable; he or she might assume that there is something bad or worthless about him or her that is the cause of the parent's irresponsibility. Many children can understand the concept that some adults are better at being moms and dads than others—rather like kids who are naturally good at sports or music but not talented in math. And most caring parents can grasp the line between character assassination and reality.

Even more serious are issues of physical and emotional abuse on the part of one parent. In our practice we rarely see the abusing parent unless the family is referred by Social Services. However, it is not uncommon to hear from a residential parent who has concerns about or suspects abuse. Physical or sexual abuse is, in some ways, easier to deal with because we are mandated to report our concerns. It is the gray areas where a parent is concerned about the possible emotional or verbal abuse, alcohol, or drug use, or sexual inappropriateness of a parent that is more difficult. Most emotionally and verbally abusive parents are not aware of the impact of their words, and in most instances they are not the clients in the office. The residential parent faces the dilemma of protecting the child from a situation that may be difficult to prove, while continuing to honor visitation agreements.

In these situations, we suggest helping the residential parent to build a safety net around the child who might be at risk. This might involve educating children about different kinds of abuse, teaching them how to call collect or use a pay phone, and making sure that they know their home phone number. In one situation, a concerned aunt who lived in the same city as the nonresidential parent helped monitor the situation and was more immediately available to the child in case of emergency.

Responsible parents who are concerned about their children are often bewildered at how the children defend and cater to a parent who is abusive. Again, parents can benefit from education about "identification with aggressor" dynamics in which the abuser is often defended and shielded.

For stepfamilies, the hot spot is the likely displacement of feelings about the aggressor onto the stepparent. We see the child's upset played out with the stepparent much more frequently than with the residential biological parent. This displacement is also seen in the relationships between residential stepchildren who have been emotionally abandoned by a biological parent. The stepparent bears the brunt of the child's anger and hurt and knowing the dynamics doesn't always help. These children often need special attention and the stepparent needs added support.

### Relationships in the Family

If a family is to survive, obviously the couple's relationship must survive. It is primarily for this reason that our initial intervention is with the couple. The potential relationship hot spots are as follows:

*Couple.* We have spoken at length about the need to foster the development of the couple's relationship. During this assessment phase the clinician is watching for signals of commitment, patterns and styles of communication, interactions that show the glue in the couple's relationship. If the couple does not have much glue—and is not willing to work hard to develop it—there is little hope that they will be able to withstand the stepfamily process.

*Relationships between the households.* When looking at the stresses and strains in the family, it is important to know about relationships between former marriage partners vis-à-vis the management of their children. Is this a relationship hot spot? Are they able or willing to talk to one another? Are they able to communicate about specific issues or do attempts to discuss children's issues dissolve into shouting and blaming matches? Do they plan well together? Has it been decided that the stepmother communicates with the biological mother because the relationship between the biological parents is too strained? Are children involved in communications between households?

Problems in these areas must be examined so that they can be addressed, and if not solved, improved. Because we are usually working with only one couple, suggestions for improving communication from their household or setting limits that will facilitate communication are offered. Referral to a stepfamily support group can be enormously helpful as other couples share how they have handled similar problems.

***Adults to children/children to adults.*** Again, what are the hot spots? Do the children carry messages from one household to the other? You may need to suggest ways of getting children out of the middle. Logistical arrangements need to be channeled through the adults until children, as adolescents, may be actively involved in negotiating changes in visitation necessitated by their social lives and plans. We are not suggesting that older children cannot be told, "Don't forget to bring back your party dress next weekend." The issue relates to whether the children are asked or coerced into carrying undesirable information and communications. "Tell Daddy if he doesn't send the support check I'll put him in jail," would be a blatant example. But many are much more subtle: "Mom doesn't recycle?" "Tell Dad to get you a new pair of cleats this weekend." "My vacation schedule got changed to the last two weeks in August. Tell Dad." Parents and stepparents need to exercise extreme caution in their comments to the children about the other household.

Many children eventually learn to shut down communications about the other family. This is self-protective and appropriate in some cases and unfortunate in others. Kids need to be able to talk about what they did over the weekend without being grilled. And often the other household tells the children, "Don't talk about anything that goes on in this house." Parents have to help children understand the subtle distinction between telling tales and sharing their lives. We often counsel families who are having difficulty communicating with the other household to keep communications very focused—for example, schedules and specific issues of concern about the children. And you will have to help them understand that although they may not like the way children are handled in the other household, they have no control or recourse unless actual neglect or abuse can be proved. The desire to have some things happen differently is, however, a lever for encouraging better communications with the other household.

***Children to children.*** Children do not necessarily enjoy the lifestyle changes that come with remarriage. Help parents remember that children can experience change as loss. Having to share a room, for example, might be viewed by the parents as giving a child the fun of having a sister she always wanted, but they forget that the child has lost privacy and physical space. The addition of a stepparent can be the loss of the dream of a parental reunion. The clinician can help parents help their children learn acceptable ways to deal with loss and change, upset and disappointment, anger and powerlessness.

Nonresidential children arrive and depart, changing the composition of the household, which can be unsettling even to flexible kids. The intermittent and interrupted nature of some stepsibling relationships means that people can't get on with the business of getting to know each other. The primary communications among children may be out of adult earshot or sight, but parents usually have a pretty good idea about these relationships and can alert the clinician to possible issues. Again, our first intervention would be to make suggestions to the parents about how to handle a problem. Only if that is not successful would we ask parents to bring in the children. Sometimes, it is an issue with which you can assist parents and children in a conjoint session discussion. Use your best judgment. There are no hard-and-fast rules.

Occasionally, good fortune joins children who love to be together. There are also children who have the worst form of chemistry with each other from day one. Then there are adolescents from different families who now live in the same house and fall in love. These are the kinds of relationship hot spots you are looking for.

**Other Issues**

In a brief intervention, there will be many facts and issues that do not come out. If the comfort level for the family and the couple has improved, there is no need to dig. In our experience we have seen couples who deal quickly and well with the stepfamily issues that are the focus of the first intervention, but return later to deal with other issues that are not stepfamily focused.

We also find that for the most part, if an issue in this other category is important our client couples will bring it to us. Again, our clients are almost all self-referred and interested in making their families work better. Cursory questions about emotional problems or substance-abuse problems in the family of origin are fine, but at this point we are assuming that if these issues exist they will surface if the couple and family do not respond to this brief intervention. Special issues, such as a child with a physical disability, a chronic illness, or some sort of learning disability, or a parent or child with an emotional, drug, or alcohol problem can sometimes be dealt with at the same time as stepfamily issues, but they almost certainly take the intervention out of the brief-therapy model. More discussion of these kinds of cases will be provided in Chapter 9, Vulnerability.

## CLINICAL EXAMPLES

The following two examples will give you an idea of the kind of information you might gather from the initial assessment intervention. This information points you toward areas that may need intervention.

### Lyn and Harry

Harry, age 39, and Lyn, age 32, were married a year ago. (See Exhibit 7.4.) Harry is the owner of a small but successful financial services firm. His first marriage, to Barbara, lasted 15 years. They had two children, Hank, age 16, and Elise, age 12. They separated amicably three years ago. Harry and Barbara have joint custody of the children, with Barbara having physical custody. Shortly after they separated they decided that it would be better for Hank to be with his father, and he came to live with Harry. Barbara remarried a year and a half ago. Elise and her mother have always had some relationship difficulties, which worsened as Elise approached adolescence. She has also been very confrontational with her stepfather, David, and was having behavior problems at school. Six months ago, all the adults agreed that Elise might benefit from living with her father.

Lyn, an advertising account executive, has a very demanding job. She had no prior marriage and no children. She reports not being particularly interested in children. She was an only child in her family of origin and reports having little experience with children. She admits to having a low threshold for clutter in the household. Lyn expected Hank to be with them; she was willing to have Elise, but was unprepared for her arrival.

Harry and Lyn seem to have a lot of glue in their relationship. They communicate well, set a high priority on spending time together, and seem committed to making the family work.

### Issues

#### COMPOSITION

1. Hank is an adolescent in departure mode. It is unlikely that he will form a strong relationship with Lyn or have much interest in connecting with this new family. Additionally, Hank has a long history in his first family.

# Genogram of Lyn and Harry

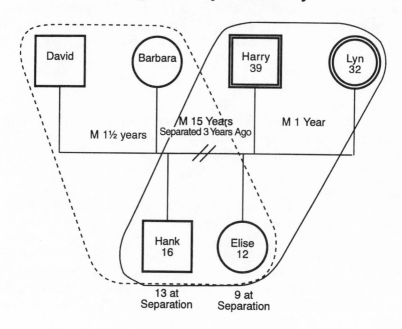

Genogram Key

| | |
|---|---|
| ○ □ | Client couple |
| ———— | Household boundary of family being seen, including children who reside there |
| - - - - - - | Boundary of household to which client couple relates, including children from that household who visit the client couple |

Exhibit 7.4. Genogram of Lyn and Harry.

2. Elise is pre-adolescent and reacting to the divorce and remarriages of her parents. Her acting out behavior at school may or may not be related to divorce and remarriage. Further evaluation may be necessary.
3. Harry's first wife, Barbara, is reported as reasonable and may be a resource.

### TIME FRAMES

1. Harry has long histories with his children.
2. Harry and Lyn have a one year marital history.

### MECHANICS

1. Mechanics appear to be uncomplicated. Harry paid his child support regularly. He and Barbara agreed, outside of court, to stop child support when both children came to live with him.
2. Changes in living arrangements were discussed and agreed upon by both households.
3. How to manage Lyn's admitted low tolerance for clutter in the household. which will be compounded by having two children in residence?

### RELATIONSHIP HOT SPOTS

1. Harry and Hank have occasional confrontations. Appears to be related to normal adolescent development rather than to stepfamily issues.
2. Hank emotionally distant with Lyn.
3. The long-standing relationship problems between Barbara and Elise may get transferred to Elise's relationship with Lyn.
4. Elise may be resentful of Dad's attentions to Lyn.
5. Harry may have unrealistic expectations about Lyn's parenting abilities and desires.
6. Lyn's role as stepmother is still unclear; this will affect her relationship with Hank and Elise.

### CLINICIAN'S SPECULATIONS ABOUT POSSIBLE AREAS NEEDING INTERVENTION

1. How can Lyn transition into a stepparent role that includes some parental duties in which she doesn't have much interest? How can she develop relationships with the children when she is not particularly interested in children?

2. How will Harry and Lyn manage and monitor adolescent behavior in their household?

3. How will Harry and Lyn manage multiple issues (Harry's need to spend time with Lyn as well as with Elise, Lyn's willingness to develop a relationship with Elise, Elise's questionable interest in relating to Lyn, family management issues brought about by children living full time with Harry and Lyn) that will probably be generated by Elise and Hank being part of the household?

4. How can Harry and Lyn maintain the positive momentum of their couple relationship?

## Donna and Steve

Donna and Steve were married 18 months ago. (See Exhibit 7.5.) Donna, age 32, was previously married for 5 years to Ken. They are the parents of Kieran, age 12, and Helen, age 8, and separated eight years ago when the children were four years and two months respectively. Both children live with Donna and Steve. Ken is described by Donna as a "no good." His child support payments are irregular and he shows up occasionally, demanding to see the children. Ken, who lives in the area, remarried six months ago to Annie, who has a daughter, Rose, age 15.

Steve, age 40, was married for 17 years to Elaine. They separated three years ago and have two children—Sam, age 16, and Meghan, age 8. Steve is a noncustodial father whose children visit his home every other weekend. On Wednesday nights, Steve takes Meghan out to dinner and Sam goes along if he wants to. Elaine has not remarried and she and Meghan are especially close. Meghan and Helen took an instant dislike to one another.

Steve and Donna do not have very good communication skills. Steve is a poor listener and has difficulty staying on target. Donna is often defensive and wounded. However, they each have a remarkable sense of humor and make each other laugh. Steve admits to occasional weekend benders, but says they happen only a couple of times a year.

### Issues

#### Composition

1. Presence of a pre-adolescent in the home. How to separate normal behavior from stepfamily issues.

2. Two same sex children of the same age.

# Genogram of Donna and Steve

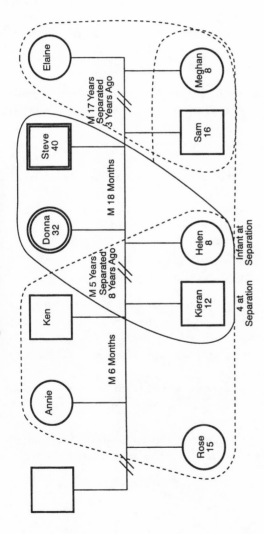

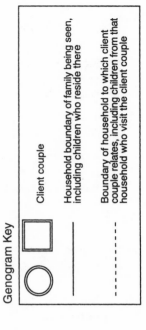

Genogram Key

Client couple

⬜ — Household boundary of family being seen, including children who reside there

⭕ ---- Boundary of household to which client couple relates, including children from that household who visit the client couple

Exhibit 7.5. Genogram of Donna and Steve.

## TIME FRAMES

1. Long relationship history and Sam's adolescence may impede his interest in being involved in the new family and the development of his relationship with Donna.
2. Helen has had little regular contact with her biological father.
3. Donna was a single parent for six and a half years.

## MECHANICS

1. Ken's irregular child support an issue for Steve even though Donna works full time.
2. Visitation by Ken is unpredictable and problematic.

## RELATIONSHIP HOT SPOTS

1. Donna has some discipline problems with Sam when he visits.
2. Bad chemistry between Donna's and Steve's eight-year-old daughters.
3. Kieran is a pre-adolescent boy who may resent Steve's attempts to parent.
4. Donna expresses concern about Steve's occasional alcoholic binges.
5. Communication problems likely between Donna and Steve's household and Annie and Ken's household.

## CLINICIAN'S SPECULATIONS ABOUT
## POSSIBLE AREAS NEEDING INTERVENTION

1. How can the relationship between Meghan and Helen be managed and fostered? What logistics are involved in sharing a room?
2. Can the couple team/parental hierarchy be improved, with Donna and Steve deciding together on household rules and implementation strategies?
3. Can Steve work toward acceptance of Donna's inability to control Ken? Can logistics around visitation and child support be changed?
4. Couple needs to work on team building, family management and communication skills as well as making couple time a priority.
5. Will evaluation of Steve's use of alcohol be included in this intervention?

## SUMMARY

The benefits of information, adjustment of expectations, and support provided in the assessment intervention may be so substantial that 28 percent of couples finished their first contact with us in two sessions. Frequently, by then the couple are expressing considerably more comfort and are ready to go back and experience the family with a normalized perspective and the idea of adjusting their beliefs about family. We frequently terminate after a few additional sessions (over 50 percent of couples finish in five sessions), suggesting that couples call us if they experience difficulty. We call this "termination with an open door," and we encourage families to use us as a resource. We often can indicate issues that may become problematic in the future. If a referral to a stepfamily support group has not yet been made, this suggestion offers the couple continued support. We may suggest that couples call us in several weeks to touch base or we may schedule an appointment for a few weeks later. We do not view cancellation of this appointment as resistance, seeing it instead as affirmation of the success of the couple's efforts. Our experience shows us that families come back to us when they need help with a new problem or another developmental issue.

# CHAPTER 8

# *Triage Assessment and Management*

When couples stay in treatment longer than one or two sessions, a more complete assessment picture begins to be developed as more history is obtained. Frequently, couples may be seen two weeks consecutively and then take a two-week breather before the third session as a way of assessing how they are managing with new information and the clinician's support for the stepfamily process.

If the work moves on to the third session, we move to a more focused intervention, introducing the concept of triage as an assessment and management tool. This tool assists couples in focusing their limited energy on achievable goals and teaches them to manage their energy in more productive ways.

## THE TRIAGE MANAGEMENT CONCEPT

Triage is a medical concept developed in World War II. When the wounded were brought to field hospitals, they were evaluated and prioritized into groups—soldiers who could survive if they were not treated immediately, soldiers who were going to die regardless of intervention, and soldiers who had a chance of survival if they were treated immediately. Our use of the triage concept in stepfamily work consists of teaching couples to evaluate family problems in terms of problems that are self-resolving (will probably change without attention), problems where energy is being wasted, and problems that may change with attention. We see no point in wasting emotional and physical energy on issues that range from the existence of a former spouse to planning elaborate meals for unappreciative stepchildren. It is much more productive to channel effort into problems that may change with attention, issues and areas where there is a reasonable chance for improvement.

Particularly in the early stages of stepfamily development, the couple need affirmation of their ability to make joint decisions, follow them through, and see positive outcomes. Using the triage concept potentiates successful change and begins to build the couple team as they successfully navigate difficult areas.

In the Step By Step model of brief therapy, triage management is based on the notion of making conscious decisions about where to spend energy. This idea probably will be new to the couples you see. We find that most couples are intrigued with the idea and many immediately grasp the concept as well as the benefits it can provide. We call these "quick study couples." Later, many tell us that this concept has proved useful to them as a life tool. "Burdened couples" usually need additional help with the concept, may have more complex situations, need skills training in other areas, or have personal problems that interfere with their use of the triage management concept. We have formalized the triage process in the Step By Step model into the triage management tool.

The triage management tool helps identify the major forces in a couple's lives so that they can select targeted issues. An angry, resentful stepmother who has a difficult relationship with a stepchild might indicate that if the child didn't ignore her so much she could be more tolerant. The clinician might ask if the stepmother would agree to initiate a greeting twice a day until the next session and report back the results. It is important to target the issue and limit goals to those with doable time frames and concrete results. In this example, the stepmother targets a change *she* can make rather than waiting for a change from the stepchild. Never target goals for someone else.

Flexible use of this resource by the clinician is important. The triage management tool can be used in session or assigned to each individual as between-session homework. It depends upon a couple's personal styles, ability to work independently, and the types of issues that need to be addressed. We encourage clinicians to customize their use of this tool to their clients.

## PURPOSE OF THE TRIAGE MANAGEMENT TOOL

We make the assumption that stepfamily couples have limited energy and time, and that their emotional resources are probably strained. The purpose of triage management in the Step By Step model is to allocate energy and resources and to foster a sense of control over some areas of their lives by helping couples clarify and focus on issues needing attention. There are four results we hope to foster by teaching couples about using triage as a management tool.

### 1. Build the Couple Team

Working together on specific issues demonstrates to a couple that they can work as a couple team. Couples frequently come to sessions feeling lost and out of control. For many couples, simply being able to agree that they will focus their energy on a limited number of problems is a huge step. To then be able to agree on how they will work on these problems provides them with a concrete example of working as a team and sets the expectation that their team efforts will continue, allowing them to build the couple partnership. When a stepparent targets a relationship goal with a stepchild it is a demonstration of care and concern to the biological parent.

### 2. Choose Workable Issues

Achieving a sequential focus on workable issues often is something that requires the help of the therapist. Couples need to be reminded that not everything must be attacked at once; it is much more satisfying to work on the achievable. By using the triage concept, unachievable or overly difficult goals are not chosen. Neither are goals where the measure of success is too far in the future ("We'll take a vacation when the kids are all through college") or not concrete enough ("I'll work on developing a better relationship with my stepson").

Until they have confidence in their ability to work together, a couple needs the reinforcement of success. By being selective in their goals, they can potentiate the probability of successful outcomes and see movement in themselves and their families.

## 3. Organize the Overwhelming

"Chunking"—breaking goals into small, sequential, concrete steps—may seem obvious to the clinician, but it is often a novel idea to couples. Focusing on the achievable by chunking issues helps to organize the overwhelming; few things are truly overwhelming when the right tools and procedures are used. We also teach that sometimes there are good reasons to make a conscious decision to ignore a problem. Problems that may benefit from being ignored are those that will either change on their own or do not justify the energy needed to address them.

## 4. Help Parents Help Children

While some children are in need of psychotherapeutic intervention, most are not. When a couple reduces their stress by organizing their own sense of being overwhelmed, they help their children as well. Adults will have more emotional and physical energy for children and children's anxiety may be alleviated as parents settle down. This helps children return sooner to desirable childhood development. Occasionally parents tell us that they have taught triage management to their children, helping children target their energy in more productive ways.

### HOW TO USE THE TRIAGE MANAGEMENT TOOL

The triage management tool (see Exhibit 8.1, pp. 117–119) can be used in a variety of ways; as a concept, in a session as a mini-lesson, as between-session homework, as a life tool to be used after this intervention is complete, and as another assessment tool for the therapist.

The initial use of the instrument involves having couples fill out the form in order to note their assessment of problem areas. The next step involves the actual application of triage management as couples decide with the clinician which areas to focus on and how to accomplish their goals. Most couples' goals are broken into steps for each member of the couple, because each needs the flexibility of interacting differently with different family members—for example, a biological child or a stepchild.

Clients are asked to mark each item as follows: 1 = problem will not change, no matter what; 2 = problem will change if addressed; 3 = problem is self-resolving (will change without being addressed); 4 = not applicable. The goal is to produce a short list of problems that probably can be changed with effort. The short list is then rank ordered.

You may want to use the following strategy with couples who get stuck on the rank-ordering step: Ask them to write each problem on their short list on a small piece of paper. Lay out their choices on a table. Give each partner $1,000 in small bills of Monopoly money and tell them to spend it on three items. This will identify three areas where workable issues can be targeted for concrete interventions with observable outcomes.

When couples identify issues that will not change but are consuming their time and energy, they should be instructed to be conscious of spending their energy more wisely. If couples are unable to do this, if one partner insists on choosing issues that are too big or have little chance of success, or sabotages plans laid out in session, you are beginning to see an individual's problem or a more fundamental difficulty between the couple. Viewed in this way, triage management is another assessment tool.

Some couples will be so burdened and lost in the complexities of their situations that it will be best to help them get organized by working on the triage management tool with them in session. We don't believe that it is necessary for many couples to fill out the whole form. Some couples grasp the idea so quickly and are so clear about changes that would make them feel better that they don't need to fill it out; just looking it over is enough.

Use your clinical judgment as to how to use this tool. We suggest that you help a couple go through the process once to see how they do. If they are able to get through the process with minimal assistance, they probably will be able to do it on their own at home and goal setting can be assigned as homework, a between-session activity.

It is interesting to us that the categories on the triage management tool seem to fall into the mechanics and relationship hot spot categories discussed in Chapter 4, Structure. It is mechanics, the nuts and bolts of daily living, and relationship hot spots, the personal interactions in the family, that offer the most obvious places to intervene in the family system. We have included an "Other" category on this tool because some areas that create problems, such as Pets, didn't seem to fit anywhere else.

**Exhibit 8.1. Triage Management Tool.**

My name_____

*Instructions:* This form is designed to help you organize your thinking about the kinds of problems you are facing in your stepfamily. It is a management tool to help you target issues on which to focus your limited energy resources.

Be specific and make your answers brief. If there is more than one issue for a given item, put down the most important one and put the other one in an "other" category.

After filling out the form, go back and mark all items with a #1 = problem will not change, no matter what; #2 = problem will change with effort; #3 = problem is self-resolving (will change without effort); or #4 = not applicable. Make a short list of all #2 issues. Rank order the list from most troublesome (#1) to least troublesome. Compare your list with your partner's and see what you notice. Decide together which issues to work on as a couple and how to focus your problem-solving efforts. Your clinician can help you think about the actions needed to accomplish your goals. You may also want to choose some individual goals.

The triage management tool may also help you recognize areas where there are few or no problems, areas with little tension, or an area you have handled successfully as an individual or couple. When you recognize these areas, congratulate yourself.

### PART ONE

I. Children: List names, ages, and primary issue for each child. Target one specific issue for each child. In some cases, there may be no issue listed for an individual child.

1._____

2._____

3._____

4._____

5._____

6._____

II. Discipline

1. Styles of discipline_____

2. My child vs. your child issues_____

3. Ability to agree on discipline issues_____

4. Follow-through on discipline issues_____

5. Other (be specific)_____

*(continued)*

III. Visitation

    1. Visitation schedules_____

    2. Effects of visitation_____

    3. Managing time during visitation_____

    4. Normal vs. Disneyland_____

    5. Other (be specific)_____

IV. Legal Issues (be brief)

    1. Custody_____

    2. Child Support_____

    3. Visitation_____

    4. Other (be specific)_____

V. Time Allocation: Circle one area of concern *or* put in order of importance, with #1 needing the most attention.

    1. Wife     _____

       My Kids     _____

       Your Kids     _____

       Me     _____

       Us     _____

       Family     _____

    2. Husband     _____

       My Kids     _____

       Your Kids     _____

       Me     _____

       Us     _____

       Family     _____

VI. Family Management Issues (note problem areas)

    1. Mornings, evenings, and weekends_____

    2. Chores_____

    3. Other (be specific)_____

### Part Two

I.  Ex-Spouses: What behavior or issues affect you, your spouse, the children, or your family life significantly?

    1. My ex-spouse_____

    2. My partner's ex-spouse_____

II. Finances: What financial issues impact you or your family?

    1. Wills_____

    2. One Pot/Two Pots (individual vs. jointly held money)_____

    3. Previous Financial Obligations_____

    4. Insurance/Retirement/Pensions_____

    5. Disclosures_____

    6. Other (be specific)_____

III. Other Issues

    1. Grandparents_____

    2. Other Relatives_____

    3. Health Issues_____

    4. Vacations_____

    5. Pets_____

    6. Couples Issues:

       Privacy_____

       Having a Child_____

    7. Other (be specific)_____

### PART THREE

I.  Your own problematic behavior or attitudes (Be specific on two items.)

    Name:_____

    1._____

    2._____

II. Your spouse's problematic behavior or attitudes (Be specific on two items.)

    Name:_____

    1._____

    2._____

## DISCUSSION OF TRIAGE MANAGEMENT TOOL

Now let's take a look at the Triage Management Tool section by section to clarify the kind of information being sought and the focus you are helping to create.

PART ONE

## I. Children

In your assessment, you want to move to the specific children's issues or behaviors that are causing problems for an individual adult, the couple, or the child. If people cannot be specific enough, they will need your help in narrowing the focus. Are the issues about a child related to the adults' comfort zone? Can you help the couple determine their joint comfort zone? (See Chapter 10, Summary of Strategies and Techniques.)

If a child presents multiple issues to the stepcouple, work on identifying one issue to focus on. Is the concern global or is it a specific issue? For example, a biological parent may identify her child's insecurity as a problem. Insecure about what? Insecurity may have specific ramifications for behavior and also may be a long-term management issue for the parents. What is being sought is a workable issue that can be targeted, an issue that lends itself to a clear and productive intervention. Insecurity is too global. A more narrow focus might include the mother targeting spending one-on-one time with her child in a skill-building activity as a way of increasing the child's confidence. The stepfather might target changing his reactions to insecure behavior displayed by the child.

## II. Discipline

### 1. Styles of Discipline

Discipline is among the most hotly contested issues in a stepfamily. We think it is important for the parental couple to be in charge of the family. However, in the stepfamily discipline must be discussed and agreed upon by the couple prior to putting it into effect. We think that the stepparent needs to take an active role in the parental hierarchy, but in most instances it seems to work best if the biological parent is responsible for disciplining his or her children and the stepparent assists with supervision and monitoring. Some exceptions may occur in stepfamilies with adolescents or where there is a compelling need for the stepparent to take charge. If discipline issues are targeted for change, help couples to be as specific as possible, with each adult having a goal appropriate to his or her relationship with the child.

Stylistic differences may be at issue. One person may be a screamer with a short fuse and the other may deliver overly long and philosophical analyses of simple transgressions. Is it assumed in the heat of battle that the child will be hung by his thumbs for six months or is all forgiven within minutes? Being a screamer is not necessarily wrong, nor is a philosophical/teaching discussion. It is more a matter of the effectiveness and the level of comfort about the style. Perhaps the styles can be balanced with each other and combined. Creative solutions are possible. Many couples must work to gain tolerance and acceptance about the differences in their parenting styles.

Most couples have to work toward finding their comfort zone about discipline, the comfortable middle ground where they can back each other up. We teach parents confronted with an out-of-the-ordinary situation requiring discipline to defer a decision until they can confer. Parents also learn that if they overreact to a situation, they can come back to the child and say, "We discussed your consequence and changed our minds. Grounding for three months is too long; you will be grounded for the next two weekends and lose phone privileges for two weeks." It can be a very effective strategy for the biological parent to tell the child the stepparent is responsible for the decision to reduce the consequence.

The clinician has the opportunity to educate parents about effective discipline styles. We often loan couples copies of the videotape, *One, Two, Three Magic* (Thomas W. Phelan),* as a way of introducing them to a style of parenting we think is beneficial to children and adults. Learning about discipline options or what are age-appropriate disciplines might also be a targeted goal.

Couples may need to be educated about the difference between authoritative and authoritarian parenting. Authoritative parenting is characterized by "higher levels of positivity and monitoring, moderate to high levels of control, and low negativity" (Heatherington & Clingempeel, 1992, p. 142). Authoritarian parenting is characterized by high control, rigid rules, and low warmth. We believe that authoritative parenting is

---

*Note: This videotape and companion book by the same name are available from A.D.D. Warehouse, 300 Northwest 70th Ave, Suite 102, Plantation, FL 33317. 954-792-8944.

best for children and families and that the monitoring (or supervision) component of authoritative parenting is particularly important. It is also an area where a stepparent can assist a biological parent at a time when it may not be appropriate to step in as a disciplinarian.

Disciplining adolescents can be particularly difficult as young people move toward more independence and autonomy, often pushing against household rules in the process. For children of all ages we believe it is vital for parents to be in charge, make the rules, and enforce the consequences. Children can be given "forced choices" about some obligations ("Here are 10 chores that need to be done on Saturday morning. Which two do you want to be your responsibility?"). Children need constructive feedback about their behavior and warm praise for their efforts and accomplishments. We also think it is important to leave room for a child to save face. This means that if the consequence for back talk is that a child must spend 10 minutes in his or her room, you may choose to ignore the door being slammed when the child enters the room.

### 2. My Child vs. Your Child Issues

The good news about each partner having a child is that each has personal parenting experience and some knowledge about the joys and frustrations of parenthood. The bad news is that it is hard not to compare children or sibling groups in terms of behavior, school performance, or how much maintenance they require.

If "your child vs. my child" is an ongoing discussion for a couple or if one partner is always comparing a stepchild unfavorably to a biological child, this may become a target for a change in an adult's behavior. These comparisons are pointless and usually are about other issues such as fairness or resentment about the amount of time, energy, and resources a particular child requires.

### 3. Ability to Agree on Discipline Issues

Couples who are unable to agree on discipline issues are probably not looking at small enough discipline matters. Most couples can agree on the big issues (such as wanting their children to be honest, have good moral values, and so on.), but they may get stuck on agreeing about what areas require discipline and what consequences are appropriate.

The reason for the need to discipline is important as well and may be the basis for the couple's disagreement. Perhaps one partner feels more strongly about a certain type of behavior than the other. Eating in the car may not be important to the wife, but certainly is worthy of her support if this is an issue for her husband.

### 4. Follow-Through on Discipline Issues

Some people are better at follow-through than others, but even where one partner does most of the enforcement in a family, it certainly works better if the other parent demonstrates support. Partners should not be shy about taking on, at times, the obligation to enforce and follow through with consequences as long as this is a joint decision and the children know the stepparent's efforts are supported by the biological parent. The rules need to be agreed upon by the couple but voiced and enforced by the biological parent at the beginning, especially with younger children. A new stepfamily with adolescents may require both parent and stepparent to take an active part in limit setting. By the time a stepfamily is two to three years old, the stepparent needs to be actively involved. If this has not happened, the clinician needs to probe why.

## III. Visitation

Visitation in the context of triage management is not a legal issue, but rather a matter of how couples accommodate themselves to the reality of visitation in their own life and the lives of the children. For some couples this is not an issue; for others, it's a major problem. The biological parent may experience visitation as a reunion, a chance to spend time with a child who is missed. The partner may experience visitation as a routine disruption or a traumatic intrusion. Visitation is often an area where a frank discussion may bring out some unspoken emotional issues for the couple, or it may be that a third party can help the couple do some rational planning about visitation.

### 1. Visitation Schedules

If both partners have children, coordination of visitation offers one of the advantages of stepfamily life—weekends with no children. And if this isn't happening, the couple should target a goal of coordinating schedules so this is possible.

The schedule itself may require examination. Flexibility and cooperation with the other household are goals to be pursued. By flexibility, we do not mean lack of planning; we mean that if a change is needed because of illness, or a relative is in from out of town, or a friend has given you Thursday night tickets for a ball game and you'd like to be able to take your daughter or son, there ought to be some give in the schedule—for everybody's sake.

Sometimes couples tell us that cooperation with the other household is impossible. Perhaps it is now, but in the future it may be possible. We have noticed that if a divorce has not been settled emotionally, former partners may be unable to be flexible. If this is true, for now flexible visitation should not be targeted as a change issue. Perhaps it can be addressed later.

## 2. Effects of Visitation

What are the effects of visitation on the children and adults in the household? Even when visitation is working well, there are logistical challenges to incorporating additional people into a household on a regular basis. If this is a problem, what could the couple do to make themselves and the children more comfortable with the changes? Suggestions can be found in a number of stepfamily books written for lay audiences. Or a couple could target attendance at a stepfamily support group in order to find out how other couples deal with this issue.

Is visitation irregular or rare because the other parent has put the children in the middle of a continuing dispute? If this is the case, a couple needs to decide if this is an issue they can do something about. If not, they should not focus energy on it right now but should understand that if the situation changes they may target this issue in the future. Sometimes, this reduces to whether a couple can tolerate the emotional and financial strain of a legal battle at this point.

## 3. Managing Time During Visitation

If management of time during visitation is an issue, it will probably appear here as well as in the time allocation category. Giving some thought to coordination and scheduling might help a lot and we continue to be surprised at how many couples react to visitation rather than planning for it. Most of us feel better if we have some control over a situation—at least we feel less like helpless bystanders. This is another area where the couple can clearly demonstrate their ability to perform as a team in problem solving. Figuring out the piece of the problem that can be targeted is where the clinician can help until the couple become more skilled at chunking.

If the issue is that during visitation times the couple doesn't get to spend time together, then making and implementing a plan for spending time together can be the targeted goal. Even if it is difficult to get time together during a visitation weekend, we remind couples that if they are able to carve out time to come to a counseling appointment they can make time to see each other.

### 4. Normal vs. Disneyland

A Disneyland Dad or Mom is a nonresidential parent who spends visitation weekends playing catch up. The time is frantically filled with one wonderful activity after another, a dizzying whirl of activities that consume time and often considerable funds, but may do little to create real relationship time for parents and children or the new family. This pattern can be very disruptive to the routine of the new household.

Dad may not know how to break away from the routine he set up as a single parent desperately trying to maintain contact with his children. A new spouse usually gets quickly fed up with this routine and often is quite vocal about the changes she would like to see. Perhaps Dad needs help with planning the weekend and setting some acceptable limits. We caution parents caught in this trap that while a Disneyland atmosphere may work with younger children it quickly unravels when the children are teens and want to spend time with their friends. Preplanning with the goal of making weekend or summer visits more reasonable can be an excellent, very specific goal that has benefits for everyone in the family and will help prevent hurt feelings, strained relationships, and misunderstandings later on.

## IV. Legal Issues

Legal issues can be long and involved, and certainly they become emotionally charged. Ventilation has its place, but the best solution for some legal issues is to limit the amount of time spent in discussing them because there is nothing to be done for now. A target goal for a father involved in a custody dispute might be, "Spend no more than 10 minutes a night bringing Maggie up to date on the custody case."

The lawyers may be in place and it may be someone's job to nudge them periodically, but often the less energy spent on legal issues the better. If the couple has a hobby of being in court, the reason for this focus should be examined. If her ex-husband (or his ex-wife) has such a hobby, it is part of the package deal and the couple has to survive and endure together. Responding to a legal threat may also be a matter of a time-to-time issue.

Sometimes the issue is making a decision to cut losses. An impartial third party can be enormously helpful in this case, helping a couple see if a custody battle, for example, will be in the child's best interest in the long run. Or will parents end up spending far more money on a legal fight than the additional $50 a month per child in increased child support that is being sought?

We encourage couples to use mediators whenever possible so that these difficult and emotionally charged issues don't get to court unless absolutely necessary.

### 1. Custody

Custody issues consume marriages. If the new marriage begins with a custody battle for one person's children, it may prevent the couple from even beginning the odyssey of stepfamily adjustment. If a couple identifies this issue as one where change is possible, they will need assistance in identifying what specific steps they want to take. They will also benefit from suggestions on how they can isolate themselves from this all-consuming issue and set aside time just for themselves. The solution to problems in this area usually does not mean more time and effort applied to the legal issues, but how to allocate time and energy to the relationships in the new family.

### 2. Child Support

She may be getting none and he may be paying lots. It can be a very divisive point for couples and there may be nothing to be done about it except working towards acceptance or finding a rationale that permits them to decide it is the price of being together. There are situations where targeting an action about child support is a reasonable goal, but goals may need to be set within specific time and money frames. There is no point in spending thousands of dollars on attorneys if someone's "ex" is a drug addict or compulsive gambler and the hope of getting back child support or support on a regular basis is nil. A couple would be better advised to take the money for lawyers and go on a cruise!

But because many things change over time, couples may want to revisit these issues at a later date. Perhaps circumstances have changed and it is now reasonable for the husband to request support from his ex-wife or to go to court for a decrease in child support. The couple's issue may be that he avoids the topic with his wife, who is pressuring for some action. Not infrequently, we see a father's reluctance to press for child support from an ex-wife as related to his fears of being denied access to his children. If children have come to live with the father but there has been no legal change in custody, a man may be resistant to opening the issue of child support for fear his ex-spouse will take the children back. At times, the targeted goal might be a meeting with an attorney to discuss options, an interim step that may help the new spouse sense that his or her feelings are being considered.

### 3. Visitation

The state has no financial interest in a parent seeing his or her children and thus does not connect visitation with child support. Many parents find it impossible to enforce their visitation rights. An examination of the issue may suggest that it needs to be left alone *for now* and that the issue will be revisited if and when the parent feels he can safely move for change. The new partner must be accepting of the need for this "for now" decision.

If there is a reasonable relationship with the other household, visitation issues probably will never be targeted as an issue requiring attention.

### V. Time Allocation

Time is both the simplest and most complex issue of all. There is never enough of this very precious commodity. In stepfamilies, work is often needed to allocate time appropriately. Many American families view themselves as deficient parents if their children's schedules are not crammed with activities, or they see their children as deprived if they do not have just as many activities as the other kids—or even more.

In a stepfamily, something has to go. The frantic activity will consume everything, including the fragile new relationship, which may seem under attack from all sides. Priorities have to be set. There needs to be time for my kids, your kids, me, us, the family, and so on.

There is space on the triage management tool for each partner to assess his or her satisfaction with the time devoted to each area. Almost unfailingly, the part that requires time to make the family survive does not get prioritized. The "us" time, the time to nurture the relationship, seems to fall to the bottom of the list after piano lessons and laundry.

In our experience, there are few couples who do not wish to target "us" time as a goal. This goal must be followed by a commitment to make the time for whatever activity is chosen. Some couples activities should wind up at the top of the triage list, and if the couple doesn't come to that conclusion, the clinician should help them arrive there. The task, then, is to help the couple be clear and specific about how they want to spend time and to make a plan for how to accomplish this goal.

## VI. Family Management Issues

In our experience as a stepfamily, raising our four children, we found that there were three times that seemed to be most stressful: getting everyone off in the morning, pre-dinner, and specific weekend times. For stepfamilies, time issues become even more complex as family members come and go (during exit and reentry because of visitation schedules) and children and adults cope with rules and rituals that differ from household to household.

The couple need to focus on workable management issues. It may be helpful to think of the family as a business that must be open to new ways of doing things, such as flex time and shared positions. We think that it is enormously helpful if the adults can be flexible about traditional roles and creative time savers, such as using paper plates and plastic glasses on weekends.

Example: One woman suddenly burst out, "You just don't get it. I get home at night and I'm tripping over you in the kitchen. Why can't you go play with the kids or something? I know you are trying to be helpful, but I unwind by cooking dinner." In this case, a father with residential children thought he was being supportive by helping in the kitchen. She was a career woman with no children, having a hard time adjusting to the chaos of family dinner time. This was easily turned into a win–win situation. The couple agreed he would spend pre-dinner time with his children while she relaxed in an "off limits" kitchen, cooking dinner. She retained the option of requesting his help, if needed.

Weekends are another matter. There may be a houseful of people or the house may be empty. A couple in a complex stepfamily might find that one set of children never seems to be away. That was our situation as Mala's boys visited their dad almost every weekend and Roger's girls, whose mother lived on the west coast, were home almost every weekend. We had to be very creative about making time for activities that would include the whole family while also making time for just the two of us. Again, if weekends are an issue, management and preplanning by the couple can help enormously. It is a matter of recognizing what changes need to be made and then focusing energy on the specific steps that move toward the targeted goal.

PART TWO

## I. Ex-Spouses

A former spouse may be a nonissue if there were no children from that marriage. In these cases, there is usually no problematic interaction. In some instances, there may be children from more than one prior marriage and additional space may have to be made on the form. If interactions with an ex-spouse are positive and cooperative, validate this success. You are looking for issues that can be targeted for change, thereby helping the couple improve their skills in working together as a team.

Sometimes, individuals will comment that the mere existence of a former spouse is the problem. This is an excellent example of a problem that will not change. Humor in this instance can be helpful and if couples are not laughing about this issue they often should be. There is nothing legal that they can do about the continuing existence of an ex-spouse. If they are wasting energy on that fact, then it must be made clear in the triage assessment that it is one of those issues that will not change and so their energy needs to be redirected.

Ventilation about ex-spouses, within limits and without the expectation that the person whose ex-spouse it is can or will do anything about it, is okay. Labeling ventilation helps keep people from getting defensive. For example, "I know you can't do anything about him, but I really need to ventilate about George's latest escapade." It goes without saying that such ventitation needs to take place out of children's hearing.

In the same way, personalities are unlikely to change and the effects of an intrusive ex-spouse must be deflected, diluted, or neutralized as much as possible. Partial successes are acceptable and represent a reality check. A helpless or maddeningly passive ex-spouse may pose as many problems as an overly aggressive one. Work toward identifying what it is possible to change. In every instance, you are looking for issues on which energy can profitably be spent.

Targeting specific behaviors is most productive. If an ex-wife calls every night at dinner time on visitation weekends, that issue can be addressed. The children may need contact with this parent, but probably not every night and definitely not at dinner time. A couple's decision to put dinner time off limits for phone calls, no matter how strenuously the children may object, is a reasonable decision, and could be set as a goal. It can be defined very specifically, for example, "We will not answer the phone from the time we sit down to dinner until everyone is excused from the table." Parents can inform the other household of the decision. This is a matter of boundaries around the new family. Children are not deprived of their ability to speak to the other parent, but they are expected to respect and follow the rules of the new household.

There is now one less interference and less upset in the family, at least after the children's opposition subsides. Children learn rules and boundaries, the stepparent feels supported, and the partnership has been strengthened as the couple successfully operated as a team—and all over one small but symbolic issue. In fact, if the clinician can help identify a symbolic issue, the effects will be felt well beyond the specific issue cited.

## II. Finances

Money is one of the big issues in many marriages. Because of a preexisting family and the financial support that must go to that household, money is an area that becomes even more complex and charged in a stepfamily. Many couples have great difficulty talking about financial issues, which often symbolize being taken care of, considered, and included as a family member. Discussing insurance, retirement, pensions, and wills seems even more difficult for stepfamily couples because spouses often have prior agreements that must be honored.

### 1. Wills

Wills need to be viewed by stepfamily couples as short-term documents that reflect the realities of *now*. A will drawn up by a member of a stepfamily while a biological parent is bound by a separation agreement can be changed once the children reach 18 or have finished their education. Encourage your clients to view wills as documents to be reviewed and changed, if necessary, every five years or less. The money spent on frequent revisions may be well spent emotionally.

Difficult issues of inheritance, such as the inclusion or not of new stepchildren or the future of a much younger wife measured against inheritance by older children, may be better suited to a mediator's office. The target goal may be scheduling the appointment with the mediator, making a time to review wills, and talking about what changes may be needed. The reason to begin by targeting the preliminary discussions is because a candid discussion of these issues is difficult.

We have heard from many second wives who marry men with more assets than they have that bringing up this issue is difficult for them because they are afraid of being perceived as golddiggers. Women with more assets than a new husband may be reluctant to share all their assets if it means that if she dies before he does the assets eventually would pass to his children. Again, the issue is finding the comfort zone and targeting concrete behaviors that will make people feel more comfortable.

Sometimes these issues are so volatile that the target goal becomes: Discuss wills in our session with Roger on June 15. Again the idea of interim solutions is useful and by its nature incorporates the notion of periodic review and possible changes.

## 2. One Pot/Two Pots

Whether the couple puts all their money together or manages things separately (one pot or two) affects how the family runs and is a matter of personal style and history. There is a wide range of solutions that are perfectly acceptable. We do not believe that one way is better than another so long as the couple is comfortable with what they choose—for now. Again, they are seeking a comfort zone. What may seem virtually insolvable to the clinician may not be so complicated if the issue is chunked out and approached with flexibility. Does it make sense to put some money together for some household bills and keep other money separate? Should a percentage of each person's monthly earnings go into a joint investment account? Don't forget that money is frequently a symbolic issue.

A one-pot system may be very efficient, but it does not allow for a number of issues. A woman who has been on her own and has gained her independence and the sense of satisfaction that goes with it may be unwilling to turn over or even share the management of her money with her husband, no matter how competent he may be. She may also want the freedom to spend her child support on her children without having to answer explicitly or implicitly to her spouse. There are a wide variety of acceptable solutions in this area. Your goal is not to tell a couple the right way, but to help them determine which resolution they can be comfortable with.

### 3. Previous Financial Obligations

These obligations can be particularly galling, especially when couples want to get on with their lives. A mortgage may be shared with an ex-spouse, or alimony may have to be paid. There are a number of unusual circumstances, but even the routine obligations, such as child support, can be annoying when things are tight or even if it is just a constant reminder of the past. Is the couple spending energy on an issue that is not changeable? This is one instance where targeting a future action can sometimes help.

> *Husband:* Six months before Jennifer turns 18, when I will no longer be bound by the separation agreement, we will visit the attorney and begin work on a new will to take effect after her 18th birthday.
>
> *Wife:* I'll take responsibility for calling the attorney and scheduling that appointment in April.

In this instance, the *acknowledgment* of something that needs to be done was just as powerful as the action itself because it acknowledged the reasonableness of the wife's concern and shared the responsibility—in this case, for making the new will.

Sometimes things can be solved, and sometimes they just must be accepted. Humor helps. One couple joked that perhaps the wife's ex-husband could send his child support check to the current husband's ex-wife and leave them out of it. The couple could then send a small check yearly to the ex-wife to settle the difference.

### 4. Insurance/Retirement/Pensions

Changes, regrets, and future encumbrances all come up in this area. How does his new wife feel when she learns that his ex-wife will be sharing his pension 20 years down the road? Both planning for future security and the acceptance of things that can't be changed are at issue here. He might also be obligated by his separation agreement to keep insurance on himself against the future of his children. Has he taken out a policy to protect his new wife, or she him? It may not be a difficult issue to solve unless he or she is now uninsurable for some reason. If he can be insured, he can rectify this situation quickly, thus showing his concern and support. A monthly check to a mutual fund, no matter how small, may be an important symbolic way to make things feel much better.

## 5. Disclosures

Is there something she has been meaning to tell him? Now might be a good time, while they have a safe place to discuss it and the help and support of a dispassionate third party. In preparing the couple to complete the triage management tool, you might find it appropriate to raise this possibility.

## III. Other Issues

Laws have been created in all 50 states giving grandparents visitation rights. When there is a divorce, what grandparents fear most is the loss of contact with their grandchildren. The greatest gift grandparents have to offer their children and grandchildren is time. If they open their hearts and their weekends, they can give a newly married couple time for themselves and assure themselves of time with grandchildren or time to get to know stepgrandchildren. But grandparents must understand that they may need to take all the children on some occasions if there are both biological grandchildren and stepgrandchildren.

The stepcouple can approach grandparents, making concrete suggestions about activities, gifts, and time spent with the grandchildren and stepgrandchildren. When grandparents consult us, we encourage them to offer themselves as a resource both to their child's new family and to the new family of their former son or daughter-in-law.

Sometimes grandparents are viewed as a problem when they do not treat grandchildren and stepgrandchildren equally. This becomes an issue when disparities are very visible, particularly on birthdays, Christmas, or Hanukkah. At this point, the biological son or daughter of the grandparent needs to take a stand and set a limit, drawing a boundary around the new family. Grandparents may certainly make financial provisions for biological grandchildren, but to be blatantly unequal when bringing gifts to children is hurtful.

Often there are issues when a spouse's parent maintains contact with a former daughter or son-in-law. We think it unreasonable for a new spouse to expect in-laws to sever contact with their grandchildren's other biological parent, but the new couple may need to educate grandparents about boundary issues.

Grandparent issues may be about money, things, or behavior. Together or in session, the couple need to clarify what the issues are and explore whether productive and supportive interventions are possible. In some instances couples may be dealing with utterly dysfunctional grandparents, and so control and containment may be the response of choice. In other cases understanding grandparents' fears and reframing grandparents as a resource can remove a source of stress and turn it into a benefit.

Other relatives, health issues, vacations, or even pets may be identified as problem issues. If these are targeted as areas to change, the couple need to choose concrete, achievable goals. If you have not previously worked with stepfamilies, don't be surprised about the kinds of issues that come up around pets. A new spouse may have no children but a beloved pet. A dog lover may have married a cat person, or someone who thinks pets are fine as long as they aren't in the house may marry someone who has always had a cat on the kitchen counter. We have come to see the struggles around pet issues as symbolic of the need for control some place in the new family and as a way of having something that belongs just to you, a pet who loves you unconditionally. Keeping a beloved pet is often crucial for children. The issue for the couple becomes how to manage the pet.

Another issue that couples may target is how to keep some food off limits from the kids. We wouldn't bring this up except that we hear it over and over again from the couples we work with (and we experienced it ourselves). A former executive director of the Stepfamily Association of America shared with Mala that as a new stepmother of two residential stepdaughters, she hid her Oreo cookies behind the water heater so she would have some when she wanted them. She had lived a single life and was used to knowing what food was available in her house. For years, Roger hid "decoy Pepsis" around the house so the kids would think that they had found his stash. He always kept some in the trunk of his car and didn't tell the children until they graduated from college.

We told this story at a workshop for stepparents once and a couple in the audience, a complex stepfamily with six children, told us that they had a refrigerator in the basement that their children didn't know about. Apparently there was a jumble of furniture left over from combining their two households and they just had to move a couch and a chair to get at the fridge and the treats they kept for themselves. This is a good example of the kind of issue that stepcouples are reluctant to share with others because they think it sounds crazy.

Couples often focus on issues of privacy and having a child together. Allocating time to privacy has already been discussed. Concrete steps to ensure privacy sometimes must be suggested by the clinician. Couples often do not think of putting a lock on their bedroom door to ensure that they will not be interrupted in private moments. However, the biological parent may want his or her child to have immediate access and a stepparent may require more privacy. The issue then becomes one of negotiating some comfort zone about this issue.

Privacy is more than a time issue and has many connotations. If this issue is targeted by someone, the clinician may have to do some searching to find out the meaning of privacy to that person. Privacy for adults in stepfamilies is not just about intimacy. It is often an issue of not wanting your partner's children lounging on your bed while they talk on the phone, using your bathroom, or borrowing your clothes. The behavior that a biological parent is used to or finds comfortable often feels invasive to the stepparent.

If couples tell us that children use their room without permission, go through their belongings, or borrow things without permission, and this behavior does not stop with reasonable effort on the part of the parents to set and enforce limits, it seems reasonable to us that some areas be locked and kept off limits. We think it is better to have a stepfather keep his tools locked up than to have ongoing contention or a physical confrontation with an adolescent boy about continued borrowing without permission. Again, this solution needs to be agreed upon by the couple, even if the agreement is a time-limited or interim solution—"We'll try this for three months and see if it helps."

If having a child is an issue targeted by a couple, the clinician will need to help them untangle all the complicated issues this may bring up for some stepcouples. Some of the ramifications of this issue have been discussed in Chapter 4, Structure. The clinician needs to remain detached in order to serve as a sounding board for the couple struggling with this issue. The resolution is not always having a child; it may be one partner's willingness to pursue what needs to be done to make conception possible.

PART THREE

## I. Your Own Problematic Behavior or Attitudes

This is an opportunity for individuals to bring out an issue that has been nagging at them but that they haven't been able to verbalize or thought nothing could be done about. "I know I get too crazy about the mess in the house on weekends and I take it out on John." Maybe John can help keep the mess under control or help clean it up if it means he doesn't have to run for cover when his wife "loses it."

"When I was a kid I helped around the house, cut the lawn, helped my father with the car. Marjorie's kid does nothing and I know I make her miserable about it." Her child may be too young to assume these responsibilities, or perhaps he's just very different from his stepfather and his stepfather's expectations need a reality check.

## II. Your Spouse's Problematic Behavior or Attitudes

"My son's father rarely sees him and he is turning to Bob for some fathering. I wish Bob would show him more attention." If this is an issue, the clinician will need to generate a discussion about the expectations of each partner. Should these expectations be changed? Perhaps changing expectations will be the targeted goal. Maybe Bob has no fathering experience and needs encouragement and some structured ideas about how to proceed in building a relationship with his stepson. If Bob targets building this relationship as a goal, he must choose very specific times and activities and both he and his wife must be realistic about the outcome. The couple need to be reminded that sometimes children are not open, just now, to such a relationship. Even if his stepson rejects his efforts, Bob's willingness to put effort in this area will almost surely enhance his marital relationship.

### CLINICAL EXAMPLES

### Clinical Example of a "Quick Study" Couple: Ginny and Fred

Ginny and Fred are an example of a quick study couple. (See Exhibit 8.2.) Ginny, 26, and Fred, a 35-year-old science teacher, have been married for one year. Fred, previously married to Ellen, was divorced two years ago after a one-year separation. Fred and Ellen have two children, Lena, age 9, and Cheryl, age 7 (ages 6 and 4 at the time of the original separation). Ginny, the assistant manager of a local bank, was not married previously and has no children. She and Fred seem to have a cooperative relationship with Ellen, who has not remarried.

Ginny and Fred felt relief after their first two sessions. They reported talking more about what they had expected when they got married and how helpful it had been to hear that what they were experiencing was normal. They clearly had heard what Roger had said about taking better

# Genogram of Ginny and Fred

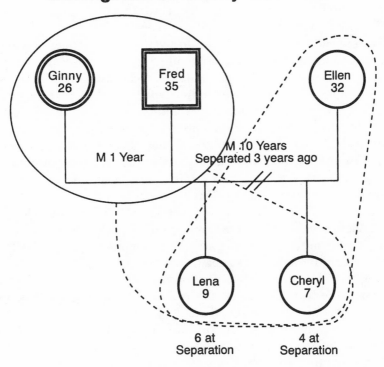

Exhibit 8.2. Genogram of Ginny and Fred.

care of their relationship and reported that after their first session they had instituted a "date" night and liked the idea of the NKT (No Kid Talk) rule. Their response to the initial two sessions demonstrated a commitment to making time to build their couple history.

Ginny had been especially comforted by reading *Stepfamilies Stepping Ahead* and the normalization of her intense emotional reactions to feeling left out when Fred's two elementary school-age daughters visited. This couple, who had immediately grasped the idea of triage, targeted weekends as a stressful time they would like to change and focused on how time could be structured on visitation weekends so that Ginny would feel more included, Fred could have time alone with his children, and Ginny and Fred could have some couple time. Broken down into concrete steps, the couple came up with a fairly elaborate plan to try out during the next visitation weekend.

It was decided that Fred would pick the girls up on Friday night and take them back on Sunday evening, giving him and his daughters some time to themselves. (In the past, Ginny had often gone along for the ride.) Ginny thought that she might use that time to go to the gym, something that seemed to get skipped on the weekends the girls were with them. Since bedtime was often a problem, Ginny suggested that Fred put the girls to bed and spend half an hour one-on-one time with one on Friday night and half an hour with the other on Saturday. Because they wanted to have a family activity, they thought that they would have a family meeting with the girls and discuss some activities that they might do as a family and make some plans that everyone could look forward to. Ginny said that she had hoped the family would go to church regularly and Roger suggested that they consider that as a possible regular family ritual, perhaps early Mass on Sunday and a special breakfast afterwards.

That left the problem of making couple time on visitation weekends, logistically more difficult because leaving the children required getting a sitter. They discussed the possibility of getting a sitter for Saturday night every other visitation weekend. Fred was somewhat uncomfortable with this idea but willing to try it. Roger asked who would call to arrange for the sitter. Fred agreed to do this task.

Roger asked what kind of couples activities they missed the most. Ginny said that she couldn't be as spontaneously affectionate when the girls were around. Fred agreed that this was something he also missed, but said he also missed just being able to sit over coffee on Saturday morning and talk. Roger asked if they made time for intimacy on the nonvisitation weekends and suggested they make an "intimacy date" on those weekends—to be used as they wanted to, so they wouldn't get resentful about the weekends the girls visited when intimacy was more difficult. He also suggested that perhaps Saturday morning might be a grownup breakfast in the dining room, with children fed before or after in the kitchen.

Roger encouraged them to view the weekend as a planned experiment that would need to be evaluated and revised depending on how it went and how everyone felt about it. In this example, one goal was to create time for the various dyads in the family as well as to make sure the family spent time together.

Roger's goal was to help this couple expand their comfort zone of tolerance as the new family spent time together. It would also help if Ginny and Fred made sure that they would have some time together as a couple on the nonvisitation weekends. During the goal-setting discussion, Roger was able to make normalization and educational input as he coached, validated their efforts during and outside the session, and supported a positive expectation about the outcome. This couple was seen four times over a period of four months.

## Clinical Example of a "Burdened" Couple: Estelle and Roy

Estelle and Roy (see Exhibit 8.3) are an example of a burdened couple, so overwhelmed with the complexity of their stepfamily situation and feeling so desperate that when Mala explained the triage concept in their third session, Roy retorted, "Then you'd better put the sheets over our faces."

This couple, who met at a 12-Step recovery program, have been married for two years. Estelle, age 32, had been married for six years to Jake. They separated when their son, Jason (now 12), was 4, and their daughter, Allison, was an infant. Estelle, Jason, and Allison lived with Estelle's mother, Nana, until Estelle and Roy married. Nana lives in the neighborhood. Jake has had drug problems, can't seem to stay steadily employed, and turns up from time to time.

Roy, age 35, was previously married to Bettina for 10 years. They separated when their daughter, Nancy (now 15), was 8. Nancy lives in the Midwest with her mother. For the last three years, Roy has been reliable about child support, but he is able to see Nancy only once a year for a couple of weeks in the summer. Roy and Bettina's marriage ended because of his alcoholism. He and Bettina are now able to co-parent reasonably well.

# Genogram of Estelle and Roy

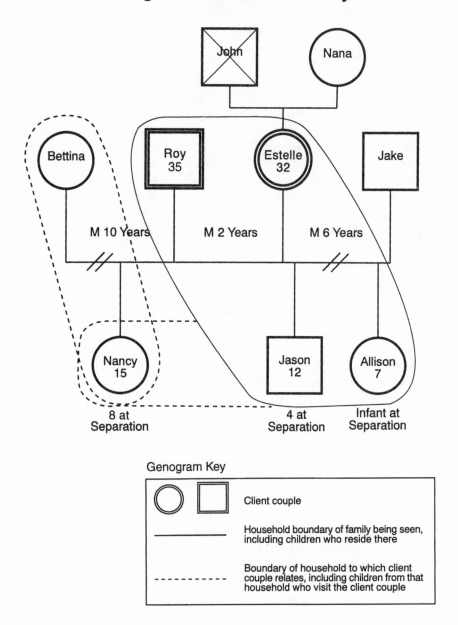

Exhibit 8.3. Genogram of Estelle and Roy.

In their session with Mala, Estelle continued, "I think we're all pretty bad off, but I guess I don't think we're dead yet. What did those doctors do when everybody was dying?"

"I think it only seems like everybody is dying," replied Mala. "It sounds like you are wondering if there is any hope for your family. I know your stepfamily situation is very complicated, but it is not the most complicated I've ever heard. Let's think together about where we could start...."

"You might as well put the sheets over our faces..." said Roy again.

"Estelle, is Roy always this hopeless?" asked Mala.

"No, I don't think so. It's just that we've just been fighting a lot lately and my Mom can't seem to stay out of our business...." She took a deep breath. "I think I'm most worried that Roy will think my kids and I are too much trouble and just get fed up and leave," she went on.

"Sounds like you're scared. Let's look at the list together and see if there are some places where we could try to figure out how to make you feel more hopeful about this family, more in control," said Mala. "Roy, would you be willing to work on this?"

"Sure, I'm here...."

Estelle and Roy filled out the triage forms as Mala explained any areas where there might be confusion. When they were finished and had rank ordered their short lists, Estelle's top three problem areas were (1) Discipline—Roy is too hard on Jason; (2) Time allocation—not enough couple time; and (3) Financial—they just get by every month because of the child support Roy sends to his ex-wife, Bettina, for Nancy.

Roy's top three problem areas were (1) Jason—he's irresponsible and shows no respect for his mother; (2) Child support—why does Estelle's ex get away without paying support?; and (3) Nancy—he'd like to have her spend more time with them.

Since Jason was an issue targeted by both Estelle and Roy the work began there. Roy said that he thought Jason was irresponsible because he couldn't be counted on to do his chores, and when he was confronted he was rude and mouthy with his mother. Estelle said that she felt overwhelmed monitoring whether Jason did his chores and then worried about how Roy responded to Jason's response to her. She also thought that getting grounded for a week was too harsh a punishment for not taking out the trash. Mala probed the issue of what kind of internalized controls Jason had and talked briefly about why Jason might be reacting as he was. She also suggested that household rules and responsibilities needed to be applicable to all the children in the household, and that Jason would certainly be more resistent to changes he perceived as targeted at him.

Mala asked, "Estelle, would you feel less overwhelmed if you and Roy agreed about what chores the kids had to do each day and what the consequences for not doing those chores would be?"

"Sure, but I think Roy won't think it's enough."

"Roy, how would you feel about this as a start?" asked Mala.

"It would be fine. What's making me nuts is that every day is the same thing and I just get fed up 'cause I don't think it will ever change."

As this couple explored consequences it became apparent that current consequences seemed to relate to who meted them out and what kind of a mood they were in, rather than specific infractions having assigned consequences. This discussion also gave Mala an opportunity to offer some educational input about what kinds of expectations stepparents have and how it often feels for the biological parent. She also was able to tell them that the most helpful thing Roy could do was assist Estelle with the supervision of the children.

When issues of respect were explored, Roy and Estelle could see that they had different ideas about the kinds of remarks and facial gestures that each felt was disrespectful. They were able to agree, for a start, that cursing and name-calling would not be allowed. Mala asked them to be conscious of modeling this behavior for the children.

They discussed consequences for this disrespectful behavior and agreed that losing TV privileges for the night of the infraction would be adequate. Initially, Roy thought that this was too lenient, but Estelle wanted to give it a try and agreed to tell the children and to enforce the rule. Mala suggested enforcement be matter-of-fact and not punitive and coached Estelle on talking to Jason about his choices in this matter. She also reminded them that Jason would probably test the rule to see if they meant it and recommended that they try this new strategy for two weeks. At their next session, they could evaluate the children's and their response.

During this conversation it became apparent that Nana was another relationship hot spot, frequently getting involved in matters of discipline, either siding with the kids or telling them to come over to her house when they had been punished. This was a problem, particularly with Jason. After years of living with Nana, Estelle said that sometimes the kids didn't know who was mom. Mala suggested that they think about some family rituals that would include Nana, in a grandparenting role, on a regular basis, and cautioned that this issue would take time to resolve.

Mala suggested that they think about how to use the times the kids spent with Nana as getaway time or date time for themselves. This might meet Nana's need to see the children and give Estelle and Roy couple's time. They said that often they had bowled together when they first met and thought that joining a Tuesday night league would be a good idea if Nana was willing to come over and watch the kids that night. Mala suggested that consequences be deferred on Nana nights, and that for the time being chores should not be assigned. She also suggested that they follow the NKT (No Kid Talk) Rule on their night out.

This family needed a lot of guidance about targeting their efforts because Estelle tended to feel overwhelmed most of the time and Roy felt pessimistic in general and about their future, specifically. Thus, choosing targeted changes was always prefaced by the question, "What would make you feel less overwhelmed?" or "What would make you feel more hopeful?" Educational input about stepfamily dynamics and skill building in a variety of areas was ongoing. Estelle and Roy were referred to a stepfamily support group that they attended regularly. This couple was seen for a total of 12 sessions over a period of 18 months.

## SUMMARY

The items on the triage management tool are a list of issues that seem to come up for many couples we have worked with. The list is not comprehensive, but it will give you guidance in thinking with your clients about the kinds of problems often confronted by stepfamilies. The triage management tool illustrates some of the major possibilities. The combinations are endless. Clinicians need to listen to the couple, who will almost always know which issues need to be targeted. However, they may be unclear as to how to chunk out the issue into manageable and achievable steps.

If a couple is assigned the triage management tool as homework and returns without having been able to focus on an issue, try to assess with them what got in the way. Was there a time problem, did they not understand what they were to do, did they try to agree on an issue but were unable to get specific enough? Sometimes couples need guidance at the beginning in making the goals small and concrete enough.

In using a triage assessment, we are in effect using an energy model because we assume the energy of the couple is limited and best applied in a focused fashion. We are identifying what is possible and targeting energy applications in sequence. Targeted goals must be set within a realistic and achievable time frame, and they must produce results that the couple can identify.

If the couple can experience success, it will help build their history of operating as a couple team. If the targeted issues cannot be changed, perhaps the couple can focus on the acceptance of the "for now" reality and agree to revisit this issue in the future. They also learn to identify self-resolving issues, those that will change with time no matter what, and therefore do not need a lot of attention. Triage management is also a way of recognizing the areas where a couple already work well together. These areas need to be validated by the clinician and celebrated by the couple.

For an overview of the triage management tool, see Exhibit 8.4 below.

```
• List issues (couple or individual issues)
• Identify the possible
• Target energy
• Limit goals:
      set reasonable goals
      establish doable time frames
      look for concrete results
• Celebrate movement
```

**Exhibit 8.4. Triage Tool for Couples.**

# CHAPTER 9

# *Vulnerability*

The assumption of normalcy drives the entire Step By Step model. Assuming the stepfamily and its members are normal, we apply a focused intervention replete with information, validation, support, and the adjustment of expectations. Movement is generally swift, in terms of both feelings of increased emotional comfort for the adults and children and improved functioning of the family. Application of energies in an effective fashion is often key to weathering the long stepfamily adjustment period successfully.

At each session, the efficacy of the intervention must be monitored. The decision about whether the Step By Step model should continue as the treatment of choice depends upon whether the clinician can see movement in terms of emotional comfort and improved couple and family functioning. Should resources be added? Do we focus on a particular member of the family, someone who clearly is not responding to our approach? Perhaps the approach has worked in general but there remain serious issues for the couple or a child. The key decisions relate to continuing this brief treatment model, utilizing other resources, or moving to a more traditional intrapsychic therapy approach.

## THE VULNERABLE COUPLE

Within a very few sessions, it should be apparent to a clinician working with a stepfamily couple if one spouse in the couple has more serious problems and needs individual attention. There can then be a decision to continue with a couple focus with the addition of an individual dimension, for example. Or the work with the couple can be reframed as being about issues, such as communication, intimacy, or an unfinished prior relationship, and not solely about stepfamily issues.

There may be countless reasons why a couple is vulnerable and cannot seem to overcome the adjustment problems before them, many of which involve life and marriage skills that need to be taught. The following are the kinds of issues troublesome to the one-third of couples who stay in treatment longer than the average eight sessions.

## Cannot Work as a Team

This issue is probably the largest impediment to success and makes the couple vulnerable to endless conflict and yet another divorce. There may be many reasons for the problem, but the clinician needs to pinpoint the reasons that impede team building because it often comes down to "no team, no marriage." When there are issues of no role models and unclear stepparent roles, there may need to be more discussion of models in a person's family of origin or a review of roles that people are now trying to develop. In stepfamilies, people assume different roles and mixes of roles with varying success. Doing so in the context of a stepfamily developmental crisis requires considerable help and encouragement, as well as support.

*Intervention:* Continue with couples work on weekly or biweekly basis. Assess communication skills, attitudes, or prior experiences that affect teamwork. Teach partnership skills. Extend triage work. Consider focused individual therapy.

## Cannot Achieve a Comfort Zone

In order to accept reality for what it is and in order to obtain some pleasure in a time of continuing adjustment, it is essential to be able to achieve a comfort zone, a range of comfort that allows a person to tolerate distress. For example, biological parents may accept some behaviors in coming to terms with the fact that their adolescent is going to be occasionally difficult to live with as they go into departure mode. Stepparents have to develop a zone of comfort around the fact that they must deal with the same adolescent unpleasantness while having little emotional bond with the child and, perhaps, no clearly redeeming facet to the relationship.

*Intervention:* Continue with couples work to give time for attitude change. Consider individual sessions with the partner having the most difficulty to assess emotional responses that prevent the achievement of a comfort zone.

## Unable to Negotiate or Compromise

Being unable to negotiate or compromise can be components of the inability to work as a team, which may be a matter of not having learned the skills or other hidden issues. It is usually best to continue with the assumption of normalcy and try to teach the skills as we would in traditional couples therapy. Again, if there is a more serious underlying problem, it will usually become highlighted and will clarify the focus and direction of treatment.

*Intervention*: Continue with couples work. Assess impediments to learning negotiation and compromise.

## A Number of Prior Marriages

Having one prior marriage is difficult enough; having multiple former marriages with children clearly adds to the complexity. Most people with many prior marriages have a tendency to explain their marriage failures as bad luck, or they offer a variety of extenuating circumstances. Multiple previous marriages are red flags to a clinician and may indicate an individual with a difficult personality, personal pathology, substance abuse, addictive behaviors, or domestic violence.

*Intervention*: Clinician needs to explore reasons for previous marriage failures.

## Infidelity

In our stepfamily sample, during the early and middle stages of adjustment we cannot think of a single family where the primary presenting issue was infidelity. Unfaithfulness in the stepfamily context typically means a failure to resolve the prior marital relationship, resulting in an inability to achieve reasonable boundaries around the new couple. It often *feels* to the new spouse that the partner is being unfaithful with his or her former spouse. As stated before, it is not the legal divorce that counts emotionally; it is whether or not the partner has an emotional divorce from the former spouse.

*Intervention*: Educate about boundary issues in stepfamilies. While continuing couples work, consider individual sessions for the person who has not finished a prior relationship. That person may make swifter movement without the new spouse present. Very occasionally, work with the previous marital couple is needed. However, this intervention must be supported by the new spouse.

## Copes Poorly with Personality Differences

Personalities are enduring patterns of personal traits that we may find endearing or unendurable. What may seem to be a source of strength or fun at the beginning may become an irritant in crisis situations. Very different personality types can get along if they are understanding of one another, but how they function together is crucial.

If you are familiar with the Myers-Briggs typological system, you may want to use this information as an educational adjunct to a longer couples intervention. Based on the writings of Carl Jung, this system refers to personality types that have no pathological bases and are descriptive of very real differences in functioning. When a Thinking type (often male) and a Feeling type (often female) marry, they may find a complementary relationship. His rules and analyses may offer a stability to her and she will help him feel with more depth and learn better how to monitor others and create harmony. He may be too focused on how it should be and try to implement rules to control the chaos. She may be hurt by the lack of harmony and her need to deal with the pain of others. They must recognize they still have much to offer each other but need an interpretation of their understandable responses. What may feel like an absurdity or a discount can be reframed as complementarity.

*Intervention:* Educate the couple on the meaning of their differences and what they have to offer each other. Encourage making benign assumptions about why a partner behaves the way he or she does.

## SUMMARY OF INTERVENTIONS FOR COUPLES

When movement in treatment ceases, as indicated by a lack of improvement in couple or family functioning or emotional comfort levels in the family, or when movement is overly slow and difficult, we look at the application of other resources.

## Extended Triage

Even if there is no serious vulnerability in the couple relationship, some couples need time to learn the skills to help them focus their energies, negotiate, compromise, and accept how things are. Spacing sessions at two-week to three-week intervals gives couples time to practice new skills.

## Traditional Couples Therapy

It may be necessary to incorporate more in-depth couples work while continuing to problem solve about stepfamily issues. The couple may need to learn life and marital skills. If this is the decision made, a more traditional couples therapy may be indicated. The clinician is advised to keep stepfamily dynamics in mind.

## Bibliotherapy

Encourage couples to read about stepfamilies. Point the way by providing suggestions and reading lists, giving reading materials such as *Stepfamilies Stepping Ahead* (Burt, 1989), or providing access to materials through the Stepfamily Association of America's Book Sales catalog. Educational materials provide ideas, support, and role models. Even though reading is a solitary activity for the most part, couples can share what they learn with each other and other family members. Encourage membership in Stepfamily Association of America,* which includes a quarterly bulletin, *Stepfamilies*, full of useful information. Recommend that parents obtain and read appropriate books about divorce and remarriage with their children.

## Support Groups

Stepfamily support groups run by organizations such as the Stepfamily Association of America or local churches benefit many couples on either a short- or a long-term basis. Some couples come away reassured by understanding that they are normal or that others have even more difficult situations. Some couples even find a new social network. Stepfamily Association of America has an annual conference that creates a supportive learning environment for stepcouples.

---

*Stepfamily Association of America, Inc., 215 Centennial Mall South, Suite 212, Lincoln, NE 68508. 1-800-735-0329.

## Individual Psychotherapy

If serious personal issues are uncovered during couples sessions, a shift to individual psychotherapy may be indicated. Among the kinds of issues that may require individual work are emotional, physical, or sexual abuse in the family of origin, or a problem that creates an impediment to the development of the couple's relationship or relationships within the stepfamily (for example, an adult with a substance abuse problem or an unresolved abandonment issue). If you continue to work with the couple, it is usually best to refer the individual to another clinician for the individual work.

## VULNERABLE FAMILIES

## Issues That May Prolong Treatment

Prolonged treatment usually occurs when families face more complexities than they can reasonably be expected to cope with. The following categories are examples of areas that create more than usual stress for stepfamilies. When a family has multiple difficult issues, they will almost certainly need more extensive intervention and will fall outside our brief treatment model. It is also important for the clinician to continually assess whether the issues are stepfamily related or should be reframed as individual or couple issues.

### *Complexity of the Logistics*

The more complicated the stepfamily, the more difficult it is going to be for the couple to handle logistics. Difficult and complicated logistics must be broken or chunked into specifics. Even so, the couple often has less energy to handle all chunks and less time to spend together to support and nurture their couple and family relationships.

*Intervention:* Focus on the couple. Teach Triage tools and format to help the couple prioritize. Emphasize effective use of energy, making sure there is couple time. Assess whether the needs of any of the children are being overlooked. Assess whether an improved relationship with the other household would ease the logistical burden.

## Number of Children

Children are not cheaper by the dozen, and a larger stepfamily is not less complicated. People combining a very large number of children take on a Herculean task. To help them understand why they are feeling so overwhelmed, suggest that they square the number of children in the family and use that number to help them recognize the increase in the number of relationships and the stress involved. Two times two is four and six times six is thirty-six.

*Intervention*: Focus on the couple. Help the couple prioritize and decide what is reasonably possible. Once the couple is stabilized, family sessions with therapist to express feelings and solve problems may be helpful. Consider sessions with stepsibling group using a focused agenda.

## Ages of the Children

Younger children may not have a firm idea of family and will more easily come to see their current family situation as just how a family is. Older children have a longer history in another family and a stronger idea of how they think their family should be. And if they are adolescent, they are in departure mode just when the adults are working to integrate a family. Stepfamilies bringing adolescents together are among the most vulnerable.

*Intervention*: Focus on the couple. The couple needs support to be authoritative parents who guide but do not necessarily confront or corner their adolescents. Work to reframe the couple's expectations; they may need education about how to handle specific age groups. Stepparents need help lowering their expectations about relationships with adolescent stepchildren. Once the couple relationship is stabilized, family sessions with a focused agenda may be useful.

## Boundaries

If for whatever reason firm boundaries around the couple and reasonable permeable boundaries around the children have not been established, or if there is significant outside pressure to breach boundaries, the couple and family are more vulnerable. No one will be able to achieve comfort and the family will feel unstable. Repeated attacks (for example, by a former spouse) on the boundary of the couple's relationship requires vigilance on the part of the couple, robbing them of energy.

*Intervention:* The couple may need to have a clear understanding of how boundaries work or what kinds of boundaries are at issue. If boundaries are being violated by a former spouse, specific strategies for dealing with this issue need to be formulated. A focused family meeting with the goal of defining boundaries around the couple and the family may be useful.

### Cultural Differences

Family members coming together do not have to be from different countries to experience culture shock and its associated stress. They can be from different parts of town, with different ideas of how life should be lived. Stepfamilies with pronounced differences must work toward an acceptance of differences as qualities that enrich their lives, offering an opportunity for learning and tolerance. Unless differences are validated and respected, they can prove very divisive for the couple and the family group.

*Intervention:* Family sessions with the goal of helping family members understand their differences and remove value judgments. Reframe diversity and differences as adding to the richness of family life.

### Religious Differences

Intolerance for religious differences can tear a couple or a family apart. Again, if these differences are viewed as a chance for diversity and enrichment they become a bonus for the family. At minimum there must be tolerance and respect.

*Intervention:* Suggest educational activities for the family as a form of enriching understanding of diverse religious backgrounds. Support the development of all religious heritages. Family sessions may be indicated once the couple is stabilized.

### Chronic Illness

The effects of chronic illnesses are not unique to stepfamilies. These can create an unusual focus for the family and take energy that might be applied elsewhere. The chronic illness of a child or adult in the stepfamily can put off adjustments that must be achieved.

*Intervention:* Educate about the effects of a chronically ill family member on a marriage and family and the impact on normal stepfamily development. Provide information about respite services for caregivers.

Assess whether the ill child or adult needs further evaluation of emotional adjustment to the illness. Provide support sessions for family members as needed.

### Substance Abuse

Another form of chronic illness, substance abuse, jeopardizes couple and family relationships. Addictions drain the family of sustenance, both in terms of the development of a child who may be abusing or an adult who cannot be a full partner.

*Intervention*: Refer the individual for assessment and appropriate treatment, which usually includes family therapy. This may mean a termination of the stepfamily work if all energies need to be directed to the substance abuse issue. Couples with abusing adolescents can benefit from the educational component of a drug treatment program. They can also build their couple team by jointly dealing with this difficult issue.

## The Most Vulnerable Families

Over time we have come to see a particular stepfamily constellation as most vulnerable, usually needing more protracted intervention that often includes treatment of multiple family members, treatment that falls outside the scope of our brief treatment model. These families, with the following constellation of characteristics, were overrepresented in our clinical population: 1) father had legal or physical custody of one or more of his children; 2) stepmother had no children of her own, thus no parenting experience; 3) father was passive or uninvolved, with the parenting burden placed on the stepmother; 4) one or more of the children were adolescent, and 5) biological mothers were irresponsible or had emotionally abandoned the children.

We do not view father custody as the problem in these families. Rather, it was father custody as an outcome of maternal abandonment or irresponsibility combined with the other characteristics cited above that constituted increased risk of dissolution of the new marriage, acting out behavior on the part of a child or risk for a depressive episode for one of the family members.

Given the information presented in previous chapters, it is understandable that any one of the above characteristics might create adjustment problems for the new family, but families with some or all of these characteristics are the families who needed prolonged treatment for months, sometimes intermittently for years. They benefited from some aspects of our brief treatment model and our philosophy of normalcy, but clearly they had problems that went beyond the scope of our average number of sessions.

When the children had been physically or emotionally abandoned by one of their parents, usually the mother (we considered the death of a parent to be experienced as an emotional abandonment) the transference of relationship problems to the stepmother was a given. These children played out their abandonment issues over and over again with the stepmother and in many cases wore out the resiliency and resolve of a dedicated stepparent. It is our clinical impression that many of these stepmothers came from families where alcoholism, some form of abuse, or affective disorder further compromised their abilities to cope. When the remaining parent, usually the father, was passive or uninvolved, we came to view these children and the stepmother at increased risk for clinical depression. Often, it was difficult to stabilize these couples enough to be able to include children in a family session, although it was not unusual to have dyadic sessions with a child or children and stepparent or to refer a child for individual treatment. In a significant number of these families, substance abuse also played a role.

*Intervention:* Couples therapy with a focus on team building and creating couples' glue, improved communication, and family management skills. The goal is to increase parenting involvement of the passive parent and support of the stepparent in defining an appropriate role. Stepmothers often need additional, intermittent support sessions, and sometimes they need individual therapy. Many children in these at-risk families need assessment and possible individual treatment in order to work through abandonment issues. Family sessions are helpful when the couple is more stable, as are dyadic sessions between family members as needed. Ongoing monitoring and assessment of possible substance abuse issues should be an integral component of treatment.

## Summary of Interventions for Vulnerable Families

The first priority is stabilizing the couple. Remember, if the couple fail, the family does not survive. Individual sessions with an adult or child, with very specific goals, may be useful depending on circumstances. Referral to another clinician or assessment of a drug, alcohol, or compulsive behavior problem may be indicated for a vulnerable family member. Sometimes, this means that stepfamily work must be put aside for a period of time. Referral to support groups, other than stepfamily groups, may be needed.

Consider bringing together different dyads in the family to work on targeted issues. Once the couple is stabilized, educated, and supported, family sessions may be useful. These sessions may start out with clearly targeted goals and can progress depending upon needs. An intermittent time frame for sessions is helpful. Clinicians need to let family members guide them to the most helpful intervals.

## VULNERABLE CHILDREN

In our clinical population, the most vulnerable children in the stepfamilies we see are those who have suffered a maternal loss, either because of a mother's death or through her emotional or physical abandonment. A skilled clinician can educate the couple about trouble signs that indicate the need for further assessment. For many of these children, we believe a complete psychological and educational evaluation, which can serve as an emotional and educational baseline, is invaluable. This baseline can help parents and clinicians more effectively assess future emotional and learning difficulties as well as a child's potential. Some of these children will need more assistance than the stepcouple is able to provide. Options might include occasional sessions with the clinician or ongoing therapy.

Children in stepfamilies who present with depression or problem behavior often are seen as the victims of the parental disruption. The clinician must obtain careful histories in order to evaluate whether a child's reaction is to the divorce and remarriage, or represents an emotional or behavioral problem present prior to the divorce. Cherlin et al. (1991) compared longitudinal studies of children's behavioral and achievement issues and suggest continuity from the period prior to the divorce. These findings support the notion that children who are in trouble after a divorce are the children who were in trouble before the divorce. We have always liked Kay Pasley's comment that functional children come from functional families and dysfunctional children come from dysfunctional families. In our opinion, this proposition holds whether or not there is a divorce or remarriage.

The children from stepfamilies whom we have seen in individual therapy seem to harbor a universal fantasy about their biological parents reuniting. The children who cope the best eventually come to accept that their parents will not reunite even though they may continue to wish for this eventuality. Even older adolescents, who have come to terms with this issue, wish for what might have been. Everyone's lives would have been simpler if the first marriage had worked. The children who hold onto the hope of parental reunion fail to adjust.

There are a number of other issues that make children vulnerable, possibly in need of specific assistance. As with other stepfamily members, some children will be more resilient than others, but it often seems to be the multiplicity of difficulties that is the best predictor of which children will experience problems. Individual therapy may be indicated in some instances, especially where children have suffered a parental death or emotional abandonment. Please note that a sympathetic, rather than empathetic, approach may serve to reinforce a child's maladaptive position rather than fostering adjustment. The most common issues for children that we encountered in our practice are included in the following section.

## Issues That May Require Special Attention

### Primary Identification Figure

Difficulty in the relationship with the primary identification figure predicts problems. We found that is not uncommon for sons living with their mothers to drift over to Dad's house during adolescence. It is less common for daughters to move to Dad's house during adolescence and this may signal trouble in the relationship with Mom that, in our experience, predicts relationship problems with a stepmother.

*Intervention:* Assist the couple in understanding the situational dynamics. Individual sessions for the child and supportive and management planning sessions for the parent and stepparent may be indicated. Ventilation sessions for the stepparent and possible individual sessions for a child are useful.

### Abandoning Parent

As noted above, the existence of a biological parent who is abandoning, neglectful, or abusive (physically, emotionally, or both) puts a child at risk for emotional problems. We see many responsible parents who are unsure of how to handle emotionally injured children whose other parent does not show up reliably for visitation, treats them harshly, or has abandoned them. The relationships of these children with their stepparents were typically highly troubled as a reflection of the trouble with the same-sex biological parent.

When a parent ceases relating to a child, children are left guessing why the break has occurred. Typically, children explain it as a result of their own bad behavior. They come to believe the abandonment was their fault, reflecting on their self-worth. They are also left with a fantasy parent against whom the stepparent is measured. No reality testing is available to this child. Abandonment is a loss for the person who abandons and for the child, often in ways that cannot be evaluated early on and are difficult to rectify later.

*Intervention:* Assess how the adults are handling this issue with the child. Educate the couple about situational dynamics. Make corrective input if necessary. Work with the child as necessary to handle self-esteem and grief issues. The child may need prolonged individual therapy or intermittent therapy, at significant developmental junctures, with a therapist of the same sex as the abandoning parent.

### Uninvolved or Neglectful Parents

Occasionally we hear a plea on the part of one parent that he or she wishes that the other parent would either get into the child's life or get out of it. Such parents see the hurt their child experiences when the other parent exists but is never quite tangible. Neglect comes in many forms and can inflict a variety of unexpected damage. Again, children may reflect negatively on their self-worth and assume that the neglect is their fault.

*Intervention:* Assess adult management and intervene with the child around fantasy and grief issues. Involve the other parent or household if possible and productive.

### Irresponsible Parents

Irresponsibility comes in many forms. It can be everything from lack of care about the child's physical safety to exposure to things to which children should not be exposed. Not showing up for visitation or doing so irregularly, even with a good reason, is hurtful to children, whose self-worth is, again, at issue. The other parent is often at a loss, trying not to engage in character assassination but not knowing how to help the child with the hurt.

*Intervention:* Assess adult management of the issue and suggest ways in which the parents can help the child. Intervene with the child if necessary for self-esteem and grief work. Involve the other parent or household if possible and potentially productive.

### Abusive Parents/Stepparents

Abuse can be either emotional or physical, or it can involve both. The literature is extensive and there is no need to focus on it here. It is clearly an issue that will require separate intervention with a child. Clinicians are mandated by law to report suspected abuse, which often puts the case in the jurisdiction of a social service agency.

Stepparents also abuse. In fact, statistically children are more at risk of being murdered, abused, and mistreated by stepparents than by biological parents (Daly & Wilson, 1992).

*Intervention*: Assess abuse and report it as mandated. Assist adults and children with reporting concerns. Refer abusive parents as necessary and mandated. Refer children for appropriate treatment.

### Warring Parents

Warring parents are another category of adults who have failed to resolve the prior marital relationship. The long-term effects of this marital war, which almost surely involves the child in one way or another, is devastating. These children frequently become casualties. The parents profess to care for the children, but in the continuing conflict the children in the end are sacrificed.

*Intervention*: Ending the war is the best intervention and often necessitates couples' intervention for the divorced parents. This may create a boundary problem for the new couple, but resolution of these issues is imperative for the child. If intervention with the parents fails, help the child navigate the battlefield.

### Multiple Losses

All stepchildren have suffered multiple losses. What needs to be assessed is the number and severity of the losses, as well as how a child adapts to change, which is experienced as a form of loss. Children who have difficulty with change are more vulnerable stepfamily members, not just because of the losses inherent in the stepfamily genesis, but also because of the constant changes inherent in being members of two households. What is manageable for one child is overwhelming for another. Some of the children carve out their own areas of control, and it is remarkable to see how some children continue to excel in school or sports in spite of very serious problems at home. Such children seem to have decided that school and, often, their friends are areas that they can control, and they put their energy and efforts into those areas.

*Intervention*: Parents may be able to assist children with recognizing areas where they have control. Individual sessions with a child can be used to teach the child more effective coping strategies for dealing with change.

## Boundary Problems

The boundary problems may be those of the child or of the parents. A child may not know whom to include or when, or parents may intrude on the other couple because they do not have a perspective on the boundaries of a child who has reentered another household.

*Intervention*: Depending on the nature of the problem, individual or family sessions may be required and may need to involve individuals outside the immediate stepfamily.

## The Rescuing Parent or Stepparent

Children need time to internalize adjustment resolutions. When parents or stepparents attempt to rescue children, they can breach intrapsychic boundaries in ways that are detrimental in the long run. Learning to adjust is a necessary life skill, as children eventually have to survive on their own. Stepparents who rescue children caught in a problematic relationship with a biological parent risk the child's adjustment as well as possibly increasing their own emotional pain. The child may need help but the stepparent may not be the person who can give it.

*Intervention*: Help the parent or stepparent step back and assist the child in appropriate ways.

## Inability to Let Go of a Parent

The child may be dependent or may simply have come to build too much of his or her world around a parent, either in a single-parent stage or because life has been so difficult. This too close parent–child relationship may interfere with the child's normal development or be disruptive to the adult marital relationship.

*Intervention*: A parent may be enmeshed with a child for his or her own reasons and the clinician may or may not be able to develop a contract around the issue. Individual help for the child or parent–child sessions may help.

### Difficult Temperament

Temperamentally difficult children come in a wide variety of types and can include those who are inflexible, highly anxious, tend toward depression, shy, impulsive, or strong-willed. As noted previously, these children may have difficulties tolerating change.

*Intervention*: Educate parents about temperament. Assist parents with management issues and the acceptance of the reality of a child's personality. Use cognitive or behavioral treatment with the child, teaching problem solving and social skills as necessary.

### Children with Special Needs

A child with special needs is not a separate issue, but part of the fabric of the developing stepfamily.

*Intervention*: Assess the stability and emotional resources of the couple to deal with a special needs child. Assist the parents in assessing appropriateness of referrals and treatment of child. Help the couple plan respite time.

**ADD/ADHD.** A child suffering from one of these disorders may have difficulty problem solving, may be a disruptive influence in the family, or may require more of a family's time or financial resources.

*Intervention*: The child would benefit from a psychological/educational and medication evaluation. The adults need education and management skills.

**Learning disabilities.** In spite of the tendency to apply labels to learning disabled children, no two are alike. They have a bewildering combination of issues that not only can be translated into learning problems but also may involve communication, perceptual, and response problems. They may have serious communication problems within the family and may process so differently that their responses and their reality may be very different from that of other children. They frequently pose complex problems.

*Intervention*: Recommend a baseline psychological/educational evaluation. Work with parents on behavioral modifiers. Medication evaluation may be appropriate.

### Substance Abusing Child

If a child is thought to have substance abuse problems, parents need to be proactive in getting the situation evaluated and securing appropriate treatment.

*Intervention*: Refer for evaluation and treatment. *Tough Love* may be a useful support group for the parents.

## Summary of Interventions for Children

Vulnerable children frequently need more time and assistance making adjustments and may have more difficulty grieving for the losses and adjusting to the changes in their lives. If assisting parents in making therapeutic responses is not enough, children may need a referral for individual therapy. A baseline psychological/educational evaluation is often appropriate. It will be helpful if the child's therapist is knowledgeable about stepfamily issues. In our clinical experience, children who experienced a maternal loss or abandonment required prolonged intervention. This is a reflection of our clinical population and does not discount the impact of paternal loss on children.

Again, the list of possible problems may be almost endless. The major issue for the clinician will be to identify a child who is not adjusting even when the Step By Step model is proving helpful to the parents and the rest of the children. It is again a matter of assuming normalcy and then seeing a child become highlighted, in need of help of a different sort. Remember, a number of these issues are clearly not stepfamily issues, but when superimposed over the background of stepfamily adjustment they become more problematic.

## VULNERABLE INDIVIDUALS

The most obvious types of individual vulnerabilities will involve mental illness. While these need to be noted and treated appropriately, there are a number of other issues that make an individual, now part of a stepfamily, particularly vulnerable.

## Issues That Require Special Attention

### Depression

The presentation of a depression by one member of the stepcouple at the beginning of treatment is not unusual or alarming. The couple's situation is realistically depressing in some ways or they would not be seeking help. When a clinical depression is present and does not quickly resolve through the use of the Step By Step model, alternative forms of treatment need to be sought.

*Intervention:* Traditional talk therapy as well as referral for a medication evaluation. Assess suicidal and homicidal risk. Decision about continuation of the couple intervention should be made in conjunction with the depressed individual's primary therapist.

### Anxiety

Anxiety disorders may or may not be obvious as an issue. Anxiety may be present in the form of catastrophizing or an inability to problem solve effectively. It can lead to confusion but the hallmark again is that there is no movement in treatment and the adaptability of the individual is impaired.

*Intervention:* Cognitive and behavioral therapies are appropriate as well as referral for medication evaluation.

### Personality Disorder

When personality disorders appear in stepfamilies, more traditional therapies are indicated. These individuals may have a limited capacity to form and tolerate relationships, to work with others, and to be intimate. If one person tends to isolate him or herself, it will be almost impossible to develop the partnership necessary to weather the lengthy stepfamily adjustment process.

*Intervention:* Refer for appropriate treatment. Make decision about continuation of stepfamily intervention with the individual's primary therapist.

### Substance Abuse

When one of the adults is focused on a substance and not on the family or the marital relationship, it is impossible for an adult partnership to develop.

*Intervention*: Refer for assessment and treatment. Make decision about continuation of stepfamily intervention in conjunction with other treatment providers.

### Adult Attention Deficit Disorder

Adult ADD has only recently received attention as mental health providers recognize that not all people outgrow ADD and the disorder may continue to be a problem in adulthood. It is difficult to develop a consistent partnership with someone who has a hard time focusing consistently and stably. This condition also affects a person's ability to remain in a stable work environment; thus, stepfamilies where adult ADD is an issue may be financially stressed at well.

*Intervention*: Refer for assessment of adult ADD.

### People Who Can't Let Go

Prior relationships have to be resolved and feelings worked through and put aside for adults to get on with their lives. If for any reason a person cannot make these changes and let go of how it has been, whether it is a relationship with a child or a former spouse that is at issue, these issues must be dealt with. Unfortunately, some people choose neurotic functioning over a new, potentially more satisfying marriage relationship.

*Intervention*: Grief work to resolve prior relationship issues and feelings about what might have been.

### Stepparents Who Have a High Need to Nurture

This person is usually in for a rude awakening. If it is a woman with no children of her own, the stepfamily experience may be particularly hurtful. If she is lucky, she may eventually get a response from at least one of her stepchildren. But she may not get it, or it may not be the response she hoped for. She will have to get her needs met elsewhere in many cases.

*Intervention*: Adjustment of expectations about getting the need to nurture met in stepfamily relationships.

### Immaturity

It takes a lot of personal resources and maturity to weather the necessary stepfamily adjustments. The person who is immature and self-centered will find it extraordinarily difficult to survive in a stepfamily.

Such a person often is incapable of being a full partner and poses additional management problems for the other spouse.

*Intervention:* Individual sessions with spouse to assess commitment to marriage and whether termination of marriage is indicated.

### Being Overly Child Oriented

To focus too strongly on the short-term needs, wishes, and demands of a child is to lose perspective on the long-term process. Children do not want much of what is happening to them when there is separation, divorce, and remarriage. They have to be helped to weather these difficulties. Too strong a focus on their short-term perspective will prevent the development of their coping skills and may impede development of the crucial marital relationship.

*Intervention:* Education about children's reactions to divorce and remarriage. Assist the parent in responding appropriately to children. Assist the couple in nurturing their relationship as well as the biological parent–child relationship.

### Being Not at All Child Oriented

This position is the flip side of that described above. Parents cannot ignore the development and needs of children any more than they can cease being a parent. What about the stepparent who is not child oriented? This is not so unusual, but it can affect the couple's relationship if the biological parent has other expectations. When there is a biological parent and a stepparent who are not child oriented, the children's genuine needs probably will be ignored.

*Intervention:* Educate about appropriate interactions with children. Explore expectations of biological parent and stepparent. Suggest activities to build relationship and family histories.

## Summary of Interventions for Individuals

Vulnerable individuals frequently need further assessment, and at times should be evaluated for medication. Spouses of these individuals may need additional support, as well as help in reality testing the soundness of the marital relationship. A greater number of issues for any one individual is likely to make stepfamily adjustment more problematic.

## SUMMARY

The vulnerability of a couple, family, child, or individual exacerbates the problems of the new family and has the potential to stall or prolong adjustment to the stepfamily situation. Additionally, specific assessment is frequently necessary to diagnose problems and, depending on findings, referral for specialized treatment may be recommended. Support of the couple and/or family members may be necessary through the evaluation and referral process and beyond. Evaluation of whether to continue with the Step By Step model should be made in consultation with other treatment providers.

# CHAPTER 10

# *Summary of Strategies and Techniques*

This chapter is intended to recap the basic theoretical underpinnings of the Step By Step model and to provide a summary of strategies and techniques you will find useful in working with stepfamilies.

## THEORETICAL ASSUMPTIONS

Normalcy of the stepfamily experience is the driving force of this model. The clinician operates from and frames all interventions using this point of view. Because the couple and their relationship is the foundation for the new family, the model focuses its initial intervention with the couple. We believe that brief, focused interventions empower the family and its members and, in many cases, can prevent more serious family disruption. Our approach is cognitive, which serves to counter and reshape the intense affect so frequently encountered in stepfamily work.

We know that stepfamilies go through a protracted adjustment period, and we have found that using an intermittent model of "time-to-time" brief, focused interventions is most effective. Implicit in any intervention is the notion of normalizing the stepfamily process and validating clients' stepfamily experience. Education about stepfamily issues during the process of the intervention is necessary and referral for group support at some stages can be extremely useful.

We believe that the Step By Step model could be usefully integrated into a variety of settings. Because of its brief intervention focus and educational foundation, it would be of help to Employee Assistance Programs which may incorrectly refer troubled stepfamily members who call for help. Churches and schools could successfully employ this model. Lay leaders could be taught the model, including the strategies and techniques, and utilize them with couples or in a workshop format, as long as they are supervised or have access to a more highly trained mental health professional.

## THE DECISION TREE CONCEPT

The decision tree used in the Step By Step model is simple: Continue to assume individual normalcy and normal stepfamily process until it is clear that this assumption about the couple or family can no longer be held. When in doubt, continue to assume normalcy rather than pathology. The therapist can continue with the Step By Step model and continue the couples model while also seeing other family members individually or in various configurations, reframing the focus of treatment as a nonstep issue, referring out to another resource, and/or adding a treatment modality. Assessment of whether the problem is stepfamily based is ongoing.

As an intervention proceeds, the clinician watches for the possible emergence of a family member who needs an intervention with a different focus. It is not uncommon for the couple to do well with minimal intervention, but to report a child who is becoming highlighted as requiring assessment and possible treatment. The presenting problem may have been stepfamily based, but what has surfaced may be a more fundamental couple's issue.

The interval between sessions needs to be considered. After the first two sessions, it is often useful to see a couple every two or three weeks, spacing sessions to give the couple time to incorporate new learning and try new strategies at home. The clinician also has the option of interspersing couples sessions with sessions having a focused agenda and including various combinations of the family.

## TERMINATION WITH AN OPEN DOOR

We view termination in the Step By Step model as an intervention strategy and call it "termination with an open door." We also take a somewhat unusual view of cancellations. Couples who have been seen several times and are reporting improvement in the couple relationship and family operations may have their next appointment scheduled for some weeks in the future. We encourage them to keep the appointment, but if they are doing well and feel they don't need to come, we are not insistent the last appointment be completed. (We do ask that they give us 24-hours notice of cancellation.) We let them know that we will be available in the future if problems arise with which they need assistance.

Thus, we encourage the couple or family to think of us as a stepfamily resource. The open door concept also means that we may encourage a couple or family to try another form of support prior to reentering treatment. If, for example, a couple has found a local stepfamily support group helpful, they might be encouraged to go back to the group meetings or, perhaps, be referred to specific reading material. This is a case-by-case decision depending on our experience with the couple or family, our view of their strengths and resources, and their description of the current problem.

## RESISTANCE

We would not view canceling a last appointment, as in the example just above, as a form of resistance. In fact, we do not tend to conceptualize lack of movement in treatment as resistance. Rather, we take a more systemic perspective. How is the lack of movement assisting the couple or family? Sometimes, the "resistance" is the reality of the time needed to internalize new beliefs and change behaviors. Papernow (1994) views most resistance or lack of movement in stepfamily therapy as based on some underlying loss, a point of view that can be explored with clients. Is the lack of movement in the new couple or family the inability to let go and grieve one of the many losses upon which stepfamilies are founded? Or is it an indication of a more fundamental couple or individual problem?

## WHAT IS HELPFUL IN THERAPY

The strategies and techniques discussed in this book evolved from our joint 15 years of therapeutic work with almost 500 stepfamilies. The types of interventions that evolved have recently been supported by research describing the kinds of problems people in stepfamilies brought to therapy and the interventions that helped the most (Pasley, Rhoden, Visher, & Visher, 1996).

In this Pasley et al. study, half of the group of 285 stepfamilies had been seen as couples, and 56 percent originally had entered therapy prior to the remarriage or in the first year of remarriage. This almost surely speaks to the difficulties of those early stages of stepfamily development, as well as to a trend we have seen in our practice over the last few years of couples seeking what we call "pre-re-marital counseling."

In this study, the issues of most concern to the participants were parenting/stepparenting concerns, stepparent–stepchild relationships, depression and anxiety, a child's behavior and academic problems and the behavior of a former spouse. These are precisely the issues targeted on our stepfamily assessment guide and the triage assessment.

What was cited by the study participants as most helpful in stepfamily therapy was very interesting. People commented that therapy gave them a safe place to talk, a place where their feelings could be heard, where they learned that they were not crazy. They also reported that validation of their feelings was extremely important. Identifying and clarifying problems in the family reduced depression, anxiety, and feelings of helplessness by giving participants a sense of control over some parts of their lives. Participants reported gaining empathy and insight about the stepfamily process when therapists gave them educational information about stepfamily dynamics, noting as particularly useful the fact that time and patience are needed. They also found specific information about dealing with various stepfamily issues very helpful, as was a focus on strengthening the stepcouple relationship. The respondents reported that the single most negative factor in therapy was therapists who didn't have enough information about stepfamilies to be helpful.

The kinds of educational information the participants found most helpful concerned the time it takes to feel like a family; clarification about stepparent roles, including the advice to go slowly; and information about the biological parent's feelings of being in the middle—all information included in *Stepfamilies Stepping Ahead*, (Burt, 1989), which we routinely give at the end of the first session in the Step By Step model, and in the educational input we make during sessions.

## INTERVENTIONS OF THE STEP BY STEP MODEL

We can organize all the interventions we have developed and that stepfamilies (in the study above) report most helpful into three categories: assessment, education, and guidance.

## Assessment

Much of this book has been about assessment and the clinician's use of the information gathered to make informed decisions about the direction and type of intervention, as well as use of assessment information to provide clients with specifics about their situation.

Don't forget to start the first session with the request, "Tell me about your situation," which usually will unleash a torrent of information. We find a journalistic approach is helpful in obtaining the information for the stepfamily assessment guide. Asking the questions "who, what, where, when, why, and how" gives you all the information you need to begin. Many of the questions about composition, structure, mechanics, and relationship hot spots will be answered while you and the clients collaborate on making a genogram of the family. The genogram becomes a handy reference tool for your use as well as a powerful visual representation of the complexities of the new family.

The triage assessment tool has been explained in depth in Chapter 8. We rarely use the entire form with clients as most quickly grasp the idea and are able to organize their thinking, with some guidance from the clinician, without resorting to categories and rank ordering. However, with some clients, you will need to start with the form and walk them through it. Especially for "burdened" couples, the ability to focus on one or two issues chosen because there is an optimal chance for a positive experience can provide important hope that changes can be made that will help them feel better about their stepfamily.

## Education

The educational or instructive component of the Step By Step model is woven throughout all interventions. Every phase of treatment, beginning with assessment, provides the clinician with many opportunities to give educational input about the stepfamily process. This cognitive approach calms fears and fosters a sense of control.

Education about stepfamily process begins in the first session with information that interprets to a couple the realities of living in a stepfamily. It is vital that the clinician be well grounded in stepfamily dynamics; otherwise, the intervention will most likely be ineffective. Because there is much information about stepfamilies in the lay press, many couples come to treatment with some knowledge base and most are eager to know how to access more information. We also view information about how parents can help their children with divorce and stepfamily transitions as an important part of the knowledge base we impart to our clients.

## Helping Families Access Information

*Bibliotherapy.* At the end of every first session we give couples a copy of *Stepfamilies Stepping Ahead* (Burt, 1989). This small, readable book, compiled and edited by Mala a number of years ago and published by Stepfamily Association of America, has important basic information about what people in stepfamilies experience and can expect. We have been told over and over again, by female clients in particular, that they go back to this book for reassurance, guidance, and to "see where we are." We do not routinely utilize the eight-step program in the book, but encourage its use as a resource when an individual targets a goal of relationship or development changes.

We provide our clients with bibliographies about stepfamily reading for adults and children, and we make recommendations. Sometimes, we give them a copy of Stepfamily Association of America's book catalog as a handy, annotated reference and resource for finding hard-to-locate books. We often recommend that parents read books about divorce and stepfamilies with their young children. There are excellent books available for children of all ages. Again, we believe that most parents can ably assist their children through these transitions if they have some guidance. Books are also useful for "instant" parents who are not familiar with typical behaviors and developmental stages of children.

*Parenting tapes.* You probably have your own favorites. We favor an authoritative parenting style and loan copies of the *One, Two, Three Magic* videotape by Thomas W. Phelan (see note on p. 121), encouraging couples to watch it together and bring questions back to their next session. It almost always generates discussion of parenting styles, useful to couples struggling with this issue, and helps parents who tend to be wishy-washy limit-setters understand why they need to be more consistent.

## Teach Management Skills

We believe that many people's lives would be enhanced if they had better life management skills, and we think that most parents could use some help with family management. In our model, discussions of family management frequently begin with giving parents permission to be parental. Perhaps it is just our client population, but we find many parents initially seem uncertain about setting, supervising, monitoring, and enforcing limits with warmth and affection for their children. Sometimes, it is this inability of the biological parent to set or supervise limits that seems to invite the stepparent into a parental role prematurely.

*Triage management.* Once clients learn this concept, explained fully in Chapter 8, as a strategy for improving their stepfamily relationships and functioning, triage management can be generalized to other parts of life and can be seen as a helpful life tool.

*Negotiation and compromise skills.* These are very important management skills for stepfamilies where there are so many different histories and realities of the right way to do something. Helping a couple establish comfort zones around particular issues is a useful concept for a clinician who is teaching negotiation and compromise.

### STEPS FOR COUPLES IN NEGOTIATION AND COMPROMISE

1. Identify your goal.
2. Find out what the other person's goal is and ask why he or she wants this or is taking this position.
3. Think collaboration and joint problem solving, not confrontation.
4. Justify your position with objective criteria.
5. Explain to your partner the positive outcomes of getting what you want.
6. Review and acknowledge negotiation/compromise efforts.

*Problem-solving skills.* This is a variation of the Negotiation and Compromise section above. The notion of chunking is inherent in using the problem-solving sequence skill, as is review of results and recognition of people's efforts.

### PROBLEM-SOLVING STEPS FOR COUPLES

1. State (define) the problem.
2. Mutually agree upon goals. (Therapist will teach negotiation and compromise here if necessary.)
3. Identify skills and solutions and what will happen if you and your partner do not compromise.
4. Practice this new skill.
5. Review and recognize efforts.

## Communication Skills

Educating couples about the gender differences in communication can be enormously helpful as it tends to remove the feeling of intentionality that women, especially, seem to often attribute to their partner's communication patterns. When needed, teach couples communication skills such as "I" statements, reflective or active listening, fair fighting principles, and empathy. Encourage couples to make benign assumptions about a partner's motivation for an action or comment and ask for clarification when they have a question.

Parents can be encouraged to teach and practice these skills with their children and stepchildren. No doubt, you will have other such skills to teach your clients. Use all your couple counseling skills and techniques. They are all applicable as long as you screen them through stepfamily process.

*Family meetings.* The parental hierarchy needs to be preserved in family meetings, so some decisions must be reserved for the adults. Otherwise, in stepfamilies with lots of children the family meeting might become a forum for weakening the appropriate parental hierarchy. Keshet (1987) indicates three functions for family meetings: 1) it gives each family member a chance to express his or her opinion, 2) it allows the parents to make some decisions in which the children have an equal part, and 3) it gives the adults a chance to remind children of what is expected of them. Expressing feelings is, of course, encouraged, but family meetings should not be allowed to turn into gripe sessions or to focus exclusively on a child who has gotten in trouble. Meetings need to have some form of closure even if this is acknowledgment that an issue is unresolved and will need to be discussed further.

When learning to have family meetings, some families have difficulty finding anything to say. A parent acting as a moderator who solicits an agenda from family members prior to the meeting may help. Some families have difficulty all talking at once. One family with elementary age children told Mala that they used a wooden spoon to designate the talker. The "talking spoon" was passed around the family and people couldn't talk until they were holding the spoon. This family reported there continued to be a lot of body language at their family meetings, but children learned to wait for their turn and not to call out. In many families, children take turns with adults as the meeting moderator and in the process learn new skills.

If you like the idea of recommending family meetings to your couple clients, suggest that having a family meeting be chosen as a goal. Families that have regularly scheduled meetings find they become a weekly or biweekly forum for all kinds of issues. It may also be useful to limit the time of the meetings. Don't forget to remind families that having a conversation with others involves taking turns.

*Devise rituals.* Families need to be intentional about creating new rituals for themselves. (See Imber-Black, Roberts, & Whiting [1988]). Often, we don't recognize that there are rituals in all parts of our lives. Janine Roberts (workshop handout, 1995) suggests the need for establishing new rituals for daily activities such as meals, bedtimes, and children's entrances and exits to and from the household. Remarriage also necessitates the re-creation in each remarried household of significant rituals around birthdays, vacations, and reunions. Other family traditions that will require re-creation are important calendar events such as Passover, Easter, and Thanksgiving, and life-cycle rituals such as christenings, bar and bat mitzvahs, confirmations, graduations, marriages, and funerals.

Roberts speaks to the differences in rituals depending on the relationship and amount of contact between households and sees rituals as a way of helping children hold memberships in two or more households. Like other clinicians who have written about this issue, she suggests creating new holiday traditions by building on top of or adding to traditions already in place.

### Refer to Support Group

Referral to a stepfamily support group, such as a local chapter of Stepfamily Association of America, can be extremely useful. Some churches have stepfamily support groups and school districts may sponsor the Strengthening Stepfamilies series (Einstein & Albert), available from American Guidance Service.* Clinicians should be aware of the support group resources in their communities and use them as adjuncts to their interventions.

The support group forum allows people to listen, to choose whether or not to participate, and to obtain valuable reality testing that provides wonderful stepfamily education. Many clients who thought that their situation was desperate come back from a stepfamily support group saying, "And I thought we had problems...." It seems that there is always

---

*American Guidance Service, 4201 Woodland Road, Circle Pines, Minnesota 55014-1796. 1-800-328-2560.

someone who has a more troublesome stepchild, ex-spouse, or couple's problem. These meetings are also extraordinarily validating because stepfamilies can talk about feelings and behaviors not readily understood by those with no stepfamily experience. Stepfamilies need to know that their experiences and feelings are shared by other stepfamilies, that their struggles, confusion, and emotional roller coaster ride are the norm rather than the exception.

Rainbows is a support group for children that runs in many schools and communities. Banana Splits is another. Many school guidance counselors run groups for children of divorce and remarriage. The clinician should find out what support group resources for children are available in the community and make these resources known to their clients.

## Guidance

A stepmother told Mala in a final session, "You know, it's like we're on a trip in the mountains, on a road with steep dropoffs. We don't know the road very well and sometimes we get awfully close to the edge, in fact, when we first came to see you, I think we were heading over. You've been there to help get us back on the road. I'm glad we'll be able to call you if we get too close to the edge again."

A guide is someone with experience and an intimate knowledge of the route, its difficulties, and its dangers. Guides often provide maps for a journey and can advise what to take and what to leave behind. Knowledgeable guides know the destination and the terrain that must be traversed. When an impediment arises on the journey, they can advise of alternate routes to ensure everyone's safe arrival.

Guiding functions performed by the stepfamily clinician include providing a context for the stepfamily process and a developmental framework for the journey, helping couples nurture their relationship, assisting them in developing the working partnership of the couple team, looking at their roles in the family, helping them to change beliefs and expectations, to grieve for the losses that predate the new family, and to target where to most effectively put their limited energy.

### Providing a Context

One of the most useful guidance functions is to provide the couple with the concept of "good enough." Neither the relationship nor the family has to be perfect—they just have to be "good enough" to allow people to be relatively comfortable, to get some of their needs met, and to hold the realistic expectation that the future will bring improvement. Becoming a stepfamily is an uncomfortable process and accepting this discomfort as part of the stepfamily context is vital.

"Slowing down the process" is also a useful concept that enables couples and individuals to understand that they don't have to do everything right away and can chunk out the pieces, working on them one at a time. One of Roger's dictums is, "When in doubt, wait." In Chapter 8, Triage Assessment and Management, we identify some problems as self-resolving. Sometimes, people's reactions need to be slowed down in order to give a problem an opportunity to resolve itself.

## Nurturing the Couple Relationship

***Help couple create a memory book.*** Stepcouples must create an imaginary memory book of their new relationship. The memory book contains lovely experiences, romantic moments, and, probably more important, memories of difficult times overcome. Because difficulties continue to crop up, it is very helpful for couples to remind themselves that they have survived similar difficulties and through these experiences learned how to problem solve and handle conflict more effectively.

***Date night.*** Utilize the concept of date nights. If a couple has not scheduled a date night for two or three weeks, suggest (or assign) that they spend the time they would have spent in a session with you having a date. Dates should follow the NKT (No Kid Talk) rule.

Some couples extend their session night by going to dinner prior to the session or going out for coffee and dessert after and continuing what they have been talking about. For some couples, the session will be the only safe place to talk. Their relationship can be nurtured by agreements to curtail discussions that threaten to get out of hand and reserve them for the session.

***Dinner at Pierre's.*** Years ago, Mala had a new young stepfamily couple in treatment. The wife had three small children and his two visited every weekend. With very little disposable income, getting a sitter and going out often was not an option, and so they began having "dinner at Pierre's." This special dinner was an at-home meal that either one could prepare (he often opted for carry out), served in the dining room with candles after the children were in bed for the night. Dinner at Pierre's became a code for this couple meaning, "We need some special time for ourselves."

Sometimes this meal was planned in advance, and sometimes it was spontaneous.

*Be creative with time management.* Encourage couples to be creative in finding time for their relationship. Most need just a little nudge, and a reminder that if they don't take care of their relationship no one else will, and the result may well be the end of this marriage. If both work (and utilize appointment books) suggest that they schedule couple time. This block of time can remain unplanned but will be available for the activity they choose.

### Developing a Couple Team

The guidance and support of the clinician for the development of the couple team includes suggestions for establishing an appropriately functioning stepparental hierarchy and reminders of the need to include consultation and review time every day and the importance of long-range planning.

We think it is helpful for new couples to collaborate on making a strategic plan each year, and possibly to work up a five-year plan as well. This allows a couple to think about what they hope to accomplish, dream about plans for the future, and set up some reasonable, workable goals for themselves as a couple team. We encourage them to evaluate their plan every three months and reorganize or reprioritize as necessary. This concrete task requires couples to spend time together—for some couples who have trouble setting aside time just for fun, this activity serves dual purposes. It also reminds couples of what they have already accomplished.

### Developing Viable Roles in the Family

The clinician helps clarify roles by asking questions and pointing out where more clarity is needed. Often, an outside observer can be more objective in labeling the functions of a role that are already being performed. Family members can think about what modifications they would like to make, but they need to be reminded and comforted by the fact that roles in stepfamilies are evolutionary.

### Changing Expectations Through Cognitive Restructuring

There is a strong cognitive component to the Step By Step model, and you will spend a lot of time discussing beliefs, expectations, and roles with your client stepfamilies. Talking to them about cognitive restructuring (reorganizing mindsets) can be useful educational input. The following checklist from Jeffrey Moss, Ph.D., one of Mala's social work colleagues, might be helpful.

### MAKING A COMMITMENT TO A CONSTRUCTIVE MINDSET

1. Postpone the need for an immediate solution.
2. Commit to a reality self-check (self-talk).
3. Define your sphere of control.
4. Brainstorm alternatives.
5. Make a decision.

### *Grieving the Losses*

Support for the grieving process is also a guidance function. Pointing out their multiple losses helps, because many people don't comprehend the layers of losses created by divorce and remarriage. Help individuals and families give themselves time and permission to grieve, to express their feelings about the loss, and assist them in devising rituals that may help with closure.

As with other guidance functions, the clinician creates a context of permission to grieve that clients carry with them into the future. This might include normalizing the common stepfamily experience of grief that is resurrected in conjunction with a pending life passage event. All too often, people think that if their divorce is settled they will not ever feel sad that it happened. Mala vividly remembers being overwhelmed with sadness at her oldest son's high school graduation—sadness for herself and for Thomas because she could not be happy *and* be married to his father. Giving people permission to grieve is a gift of great worth.

### *Target Where to Place Their Energy*

Giving guidance in choosing appropriate targets for behavior change helps the couple feel more in control and lessens feelings of depression and anxiety we see so often in our stepfamily clients. The clinician listens to what changes the couple would find most useful or comforting and guides the selection process based on his or her knowledge about stepfamilies. Because energy is in short supply in stepfamilies and must be used wisely, the clinician's objectivity in this area will be a big help in choosing areas where progress can be made with maximum benefit.

## SUGGESTIONS FOR THERAPISTS

1. *Assume a moment in time.* Your assessment is based on a snapshot of this family at this time, but remember that stepfamilies are "works in progress."
2. *Validate efforts.* The efforts of adults and children in the new family need to be validated by the clinician through verbal pats on the back. Often stepparents experience little payoff for their efforts with stepchildren and need recognition by the clinician, who models this behavior for the spouse.
3. *Help couples remember why they married.* Asking a difficult couple about how they met, why they fell in love, gives a benchmark for the kind of feelings to which couples hope to return. Often, couples feel so overwhelmed that they forget why they got married.
4. *Use humor.* Stepcouples who maintain a sense of humor have a decided advantage. Many ridiculous things that happen in stepfamilies can be turned into either emotional conflagrations or reasons to laugh. It is much better to encourage couples to laugh about the absurd. Laughter can contribute to social cohesion and to feeling like part of the in-group—certainly a feeling we want to promote in stepfamilies.
5. *Don't push families into premature cohesion.* Stepfamilies need time to build relationships, and pushing them to be more cohesive than they are ready to be sends a signal that they aren't doing stepfamily right or fast enough.
6. *Maintain a future orientation.* Help couples get outside of how the "now" moment feels and plan for the future.
7. *Support relationships between households.* This may not happen during this brief intervention, but letting couples know that it can happen and is something to be worked toward primes them to be more accepting of the possibility.
8. *Don't take sides except....* While it is important for clinicians to remain objective and not fall into a couple's blame game, being objective does not mean not being empathetic to a couple who are experiencing difficulties with a former spouse. We think that this focus on a difficult "ex" sometimes may be part of a couple's need to strengthen the boundary around their relationship.
9. *Encourage interim solutions.* Solutions that work for now and are good enough for now are just fine. As the family and relationships evolve, new solutions will evolve as well.

10. *Use of self.* It should be obvious by now that both Mala and Roger have very interactive therapeutic styles. If you are part of a stepfamily, disclose your stepfamily experience to clients. It will give you credibility. Mala and Roger call themselves "stepfamily veterans" and speak about the positive parts of their stepfamily, giving hope to discouraged clients. They are conscious of being viewed as role models to the couple. They also tell funny stories, some of their personal reactions to being in a stepfamily, and the difficult hurdles they had to overcome. They also laugh about how naive they were, how unprepared, and what would have helped. This creates a context of hope for getting through the hard times—if we can do it, so can you—and levels the playing field.

    Two caveats: First, if clinicians are stepfamily members, they need to be aware of their own stepfamily issues so they don't identify inappropriately with one member of the couple or with an issue being confronted. And second, with some stepfamilies you will know that it is not appropriate to use information about yourself. This is a judgment based on each clinician's experience.

11. *Clarify and highlight issues.* Is the issue presented a stepfamily issue or something else? Are concerns about a child reasonable or a reflection of normal behavior?

12. *Play from your therapeutic strengths.* Incorporate the Step By Step model into your style of working. Continue to be who you are and do what works for you as long as you remember to screen interventions through a solid understanding of stepfamily dynamics.

13. *Look for symbolic issues.* Small issues that don't get resolved are most likely rooted in some symbolic issue; until that is uncovered, movement may not be possible. Identifying symbolic issues that can be productively targeted for change creates a powerful intervention.

14. *Help parents help their children.* Remind parents that children may be assisted in their transition from household to household by carrying transitional objects, acknowledging their membership in two families, and assisting them with contact with the other household. This could involve dialing a phone number for a small child or mailing a letter or drawing.

15. *Encourage change beyond the intervention.* Recommend attendance at a stepfamily support group and specific reading for issues

that may be problematic in the future. Also, encourage the couple to continue to make couple time a priority—a deposit to their marital bank account so they'll have something to draw on during a crisis.

## SUMMARY

Much of the strength of the Step By Step model lies in its simplicity. It is also a collaborative model, creating a synergistic effort between the clinician and the clients. Even though the clinician does not expect to stay with a family throughout the stepfamily developmental sequence, the assessment, education, and guidance provided to the family in this brief intervention gives them a map of the journey and helps them better understand and feel good enough about the process to tolerate the difficult—and at times uncomfortable—transitions they will encounter as their stepfamily evolves.

# CHAPTER 11

# *Successful Stepfamilies*

The Step By Step model assumes that stepfamilies are normal and can be successful in a variety of ways, enriching the lives of their members. Our view about stepfamilies is not about psychopathology, but about adjustment and how people can make it through a complex and difficult developmental process that takes years to navigate. The issue is not just about getting through, surviving, but also about what family members gain from the experience.

The stepfamily functions differently from other forms of families and has its own strengths. The couple and the individual family members learn useful skills and develop views and abilities that help them with other challenging life experiences. What follows is our view of the characteristics of the couple, the children, and the family who successfully navigate the stepfamily journey.

## SUCCESSFUL STEPCOUPLES

The successful stepcouple:

- Assume that, through their partnership, they can weather the storm.
- Believe in all the children.
- Are devoted to each other.
- Demonstrate commitment and staying power.
- Are patient, laugh together, and maintain hope for the future.
- Are flexible, accepting "for now" and "good enough" solutions.
- Become better communicators and creative problem solvers.
- Appreciate their partners for who they are and for their unique contributions.

- Know that love *will* conquer all if they get education, support, and guidance about their stepfamily.

## SUCCESSFUL STEPCHILDREN

Successful stepchildren:

- Carve out territories they can clearly affect, such as school and peers, regardless of what is happening in their family.
- Focus on competence, develop expertise, and find success in selected areas.
- Learn to assert themselves.
- Screen their communications, learning what are productive communications between households.
- Come to terms with children's universal fantasy about parental reconciliation.
- Learn about their strengths and ability to overcome adversity.
- Develop a sense of strength and resourcefulness that stands them in good stead as they move forward in their lives.

## SUCCESSFUL STEPFAMILIES

The successful stepfamily:

- Accepts, nurtures, welcomes, and celebrates all family members.
- Looks for creative solutions.
- Celebrates the diversity and uniqueness of each family member.
- Accepts and grows from its losses.
- Accepts each person for who he or she is.
- Is flexible, looks to the future, and moves forward.

# References

Anderson, J.Z., & White, G.D. (1986). An empirical investigation of relation-ship patterns in functional and dysfunctional nuclear families and stepfamilies. *Family Process, 25,* 407–422.

Bernstein, A. C. (1989). *Yours, mine, and ours.* New York: Scribner.

Browning, S. (1994). Treating stepfamilies: Alternatives to traditional family therapy. In K. Pasley & M. Ihinger-Tallman (Eds.), *Stepparenting: Issues in theory, research and practice.* Westport, CT: Praeger.

Budman, S. (1990). The myth of termination in brief therapy: Or, It ain't over till it's over. In J.K. Zeig (Ed.), *Brief therapy: Myths, methods and metaphors.* New York: Brunner/Mazel.

Burt, M. (Ed.) (1989). *Stepfamilies stepping ahead.* Lincoln, NE: Stepfamilies Press.

Cherlin, A.J., Furstenberg, F.F., Jr., Chase–Lansdale, P.L., Kieran, K.E., Robins, P.K., Morrison, D.R., & Teitler, J.O. (1991). Longitudinal studies of effects of divorce on children in Great Britain and the United States. *Science, 252,* 1386–1389.

Clingempeel, W.G., Brand, E., & Ievoli, R. (1984). Stepparent–stepchild rela-tions in stepmother and stepfather families: A multimethod study. *Family Relations, 33,* 465–473.

Cummings, N. (1990). Brief intermittent psychotherapy throughout the life cycle. In J. K. Zeig (Ed.), *Brief therapy: Myths, methods and metaphors.* New York: Brunner/Mazel.

Daly, M., & Wilson, M. (1992). Cinderella. *Harvard Mental Health Letter, 9,* 5–7.

Einstein, E. (1982). *Stepfamilies: Living, loving and learning.* New York: MacMillan.

Heatherington, E.M. (1987). Family relations six years after divorce. In K. Pasley & M. Ihinger–Tallman (Eds.), *Remarriage and stepparenting: Current research and theory.* New York: Guilford.

Heatherington, E.M., & Clingempeel, W.G. (1992). Coping with marital transi-tions: A family systems perspective. *Monographs of the Society for Research in Child Development, 57,* 2–3.

Imber–Black, E., Roberts, J., & Whiting, R. (1988). *Rituals in families and family therapy.* New York: Norton.

Keshet, J. (1987). *Love and power in the stepfamily.* New York: McGraw–Hill.

Kimmel, D.C. (1974). *Adulthood and aging.* New York: Wiley.

McGoldrick, M., & Gerson, R. (1985). *Genograms in family assessment.* New York: Norton.

Miller, J. B. (1976). *Toward a new psychology of women.* Boston: Beacon Press.

Papernow, P. L. (1994). *Becoming a stepfamily.* San Francisco: Jossey-Bass.

Pasley, K. (1994). What is effective stepparenting? *Stepfamilies, 14*(2), 5–6.

Pasley, K., & Ihinger–Tallman, M. (Eds.). (1994). *Stepparenting: Issues in theory, research and practice.* Westport, CT: Praeger.

Pasley, K., Rhoden, L., Visher, E., & Visher, J. (1996). Stepfamilies in therapy: Insights from adult stepfamily members. *Journal of Marriage and Family Therapy, 22*(3), 343–357.

Sager, C.J., Brown, H.S., Crohn, H., Engel, T., Rodstein, E., & Walker, L. (1983). *Treating the remarried family.* New York: Brunner/Mazel.

Sheehy, G. (1984). *Passages.* New York: Bantam.

Visher, E.B., & Visher, J.S. (1980). *Stepfamilies: Myths and realities.* Secaucus: Citadel Press.

Visher, E.B., & Visher, J.S. (1988). *Old loyalties, new ties.* New York: Brunner/Mazel.

Zeig, J.K. (Ed.) 1990, *Brief Therapy: Myths, methods and metaphors.* New York: Brunner/Mazel.

# Index

financial factors, 130–133
grandparents, 133–134
privacy, 134–135
problematic behaviors, 135–136
purpose of, 114–115
relatives, 133–134
time allocation, 127–128
use of, 115–119

Unrealistic expectations, 55–59

Ventilation, Stepfamily Assessment
    Guide, techniques, 88–89
Visher, E. B., 4, 12, 18, 55, 65, 70, 72,
    168
Visher, J. S., 4, 12, 18, 55, 65, 70, 72, 168
Visitation rights
  family structure mechanics, 48
  Stepfamily Assessment Guide,
    95–97

triage management tool, 123–125,
    127
Vulnerability, 145–165
  of children, 155–161
  of couples, 145–150
  of families, 150–155
  individual, 161–164

Warring parents, child vulnerability, 158
White, G. D., 61
Whiting, R., 76, 174
Widow/widower remarriage, expecta-
    tions, 66–67
Wills, triage management tool,
    130–131
Wilson, M., 63, 158
Women, stepmothers, relationship
    issues, 52

Zeig, J. K., 5